MW01644383

All Scripture quotations, unless otherwise indicated, are taken from the King James Version.

To give reverence all names referring to Jesus Christ are capitalized.

∞∞∞

Romans 8:37 *New King James Version Yet in all these things we are more than conquerors through Him who loved us.*

Have you ever stood by the bedside of a loved one to say good-bye too soon?

Have you ever faced a diagnosis that changed your life?

Have you ever been to a funeral of a precious child?

Only Jesus Christ can allow you to see beauty in brokenness.

Only Jesus Christ can bring beauty out of ashes.

Come and let's walk together as you read Footprints to a Miracle.

∞∞∞

Reviews

This book is written with powerful insight and conviction. Footprints to a Miracle give an account of God touching and transforming Olivia's life from a victim to a victorious person in Jesus Christ.

Barbara Barfield-Jackson
Retired Educator
Alcalu, South Carolina

This book "Footprints to a Miracle" is very inspiring and captivating.

Melissa Green
Educator
Florence, South Carolin

Preface

I have written this book depending only on Jesus Christ who gave this mandate: "And the LORD answered me, and said, Write the vision, and make it plain upon tables, that he may run that readeth it. For the vision is yet for an appointed time, but at the end it shall speak, and not lie; though it tarry, wait for it; because it will surely come, it will not tarry" (Habakkuk 2:2-3).

The power of God has been with me throughout the time of putting my story on paper, and the power of the Lord has been revealed in my life. "Who hath believed our report? and to whom is the arm of the LORD revealed?" (Isaiah 53:1)

I faced many struggles writing this memoir, struggles within and without. I feared sharing the most intimate details and the heart-wrenching circumstances of my life. I walk through life's seasons of pain and glory. I openly share my secrets, as my life becomes an open book. In the process of writing, I shouted many times, "I give up. I can't take any more." I grumbled and complained. When I was at my weakest, God comforted my heart and gave me the inspiration to write. The core and purpose of this book is found in 2 Corinthians 1:3-4: "Blessed be God, even the Father of our Lord Jesus Christ, the Father of mercies, and the God of all comfort; Who comforteth us in all our tribulation, that we may be able to comfort them which are in any trouble, by the comfort wherewith we ourselves are comforted of God." Therefore, I write, hoping to pass on to you the same comfort I received from Jesus Christ.

Every step of my life, up to the present time, has been a miracle walk--a life of great pain, yet a miracle walk. A life with a broken heart and broken dreams, yet a miracle walk. A walk with grave attacks on my health, yet a miracle walk. I write sharing the fragments gathered through different seasons of my life. In each season, I experienced God's miracle-working healing power in the middle of a miracle walk.

My family and friends where I have lived and where I worship have all been valuable in writing this memoir. My husband, Samuel, gave me the title *Footprints to a Miracle*. I began to write under the powerful force of God's anointing, journeying through lessons lived and learned. The Holy Spirit opened the window of my heart, and I entered territory I once dared not to speak or think about. Jesus Christ, the anchor of my soul, gave me hope as I entered a place filled with hidden insecurities: "Which hope we have as an anchor of the soul, both sure and stedfast, and which entereth into that within the veil" (Heb. 6: 19).

I have made unwise decisions in my past, but God has remained faithful. As a child of God I have rested in Romans 8:28: "And we know that all things work together for good to them that love God, to them who are the called according to his purpose."

I have mentally relived my agonizing past in order to share with others. Through Jesus Christ, I have felt deep emotional healing take place in my life as my past resurfaced through my writing. I have chosen to open the windows of my soul and to share my life. My destination is heaven and to see Jesus face-to-face, and my ultimate goal is to stay in the race looking to Jesus: "Let us run with patience the race that is set before us, Looking unto Jesus the author and finisher of our faith" (Heb. 12:1-2). I pray that as you read this book, you will feel the strength of its message of hope and love through the power of the Holy Spirit. My story is important not because it is mine. I write, in truth believing, that my yesterdays can help someone in his or her today.

Table of Contents

Looking From the Inside Out

∞∞∞

Behold, thou desirest truth in the inward parts: and in the hidden part thou shalt make me to know wisdom.Psalm 51:6

One October day in the fall of 1996, when the greenery of spring and summer had changed to the oranges, reds, and yellows of the fall, I realized I too was changing. I sat on my bed asking myself, "Who am I and how have I survived?" I became overwhelmed with emotion as tears began rolling down my face, but these tears were different from the tears of self-pity I had shed before. As I wiped the tears from my eyes, I looked at myself in the mirror; and at that very moment it seemed as if time stood still. My physical senses heightened to the point where I began to seemingly taste, smell, touch, hear, and see the past events of my life. My mind was filled with this unveiled revelation of my miracle walk with God, my heart and spirit echoed, I must share the story that had unfolded within. I immediately went to my computer to begin the imparting of my life's journey:

In this account of my life's journey, I compare my life to the changing of the seasons. The author of Ecclesiastes writes, "To every thing there is a season, and a time for every purpose under the heaven: A time to be born, and a time to die; a time to plant, and a time to pluck up that which is planted" (Eccl. 3:1-2).

Every season has an appointed time, and I believe this applies to spiritual seasons as well. I experience winter as a time to break down, a time to weep, and a time to mourn life's heartbreaking experiences. Spring for me stands for a time to heal and a time to build. Summer represents a time to laugh, dance, and renew my mind. Fall becomes a time to remove the worn and to gather in the lessons learned. Each season of my spiritual walk is filled with purpose.

I experience these seasons believing that Jesus will bring me through and carry me into each one: "And He changes the times and the seasons; He removes kings and raises up kings; He gives wisdom to the wise and knowledge to those who have understanding" (Dan. 2:21 NKJV).

On that day, when I sat at my computer desk with a grateful heart to begin writing my life's story, I began to talk to Jesus. "Jesus," I cried, "in the winter season I felt the cold and the winds of trouble blow, overwhelming me with grief and pain. In the spring season, life emerged from within my soul as you healed my broken heart. And again in the summer, you filled my life with laughter, after the devil tried to destroy me. In the fall of my life, I crucified my will and my flesh. Dear Jesus, please forgive me for the times I stayed too long in the winter season. I experienced change in every season, and I am not the same. Jesus, I thank you for always moving me into a new season." After praying and talking to Jesus, I felt peace within my heart and spirit, and ready to share my life's story.

The Journey Begins

∞∞∞

Before I formed thee in the belly I knew thee; and before thou camest forth out of the womb I sanctified thee, and I ordained thee a prophet unto the nations.
Jeremiah 1:5

My life began as a miracle. I entered the world early, through a premature birth, on February 11, 1959, in South Carolina. A local midwife, Mrs. McNeil, assisted my mother during this time. I weighed two pounds and two ounces. When I got older, I could not comprehend my birth weight. My father said, "You were so small and no bigger than my hand." My mother said, "You were so little and had silky black hair." My parents called me their miracle child because they did not expect me to live.

I grew up in a small rural community called Evergreen, in Florence County, South Carolina. I am the oldest daughter, the middle child, with two older brothers and two younger sisters. In our community, it was not just a saying, but a practice that "It takes a village to raise a child." I had so many influences that I liken my life to a patchwork quilt sewn together with different pieces of material.

In my earlier years, I lived in a simple two bedroom, wood-frame house. My father later constructed a larger house with four bedrooms.

My father was a hardworking man. He provided for our family by working as a laborer and later became a foreman for a lumber company until his retirement. My mother also worked outside the home at times as a domestic worker and a factory worker. She later entered the nursing field as a nurse's assistant, the job from which she retired.

I would ponder, "Was my family poor?" Later in life, I asked my brothers and sisters this question and their opinions varied. But we all agreed we were survivors and that our parents, with God's help, were able to take a little and make much. Their main objective of our father and mother was to provide for our family. They provided material things and intrinsic values, providing us with our needs and some of our desires.

My memory of my childhood is that my parents were good role models and provided the spiritual inheritance that formed the foundation for my life. My family blood lineage is comprised of men and women of God. My father and grandmother were preachers as were others within my family lineage. My family provided the examples of strength and perseverance I needed to survive life's challenges. My father, being a man of biblical principles, raised his children with godly standards. In our home, we went to church every Sunday, and we were not given a choice.

At an early age, I demonstrated a sense of maturity. As the oldest girl, my parents expected much of me. I would babysit my younger sisters, and at times I would prepare dinner, and I helped keep the house clean. My parents set the guidelines and rules of our home, but as a typical teenager, I challenged my parents' authority. Through rebellion and peer pressure, I sought to find my own identity.

In 1970, a desegregation plan for the state's schools was implemented in South Carolina. This presented me with challenges I had never experienced before. I overcame the racial barriers that separated the people of our community by adhering to my parents' philosophies for living in an imperfect world. They held strongly to the viewpoint that you needed to treat people the way you wanted to be treated. I realized that their firm beliefs helped me to survive.

I dated only occasionally in my teen years. As I look back, however, I don't feel as if I missed it too much. In 1973 I met my first love, Wayne Daniels. Wayne was a very intelligent and carefree person. We lived about twenty miles apart, and got involved with each other through family members and church life. We started dating, fell in love, and remained sweethearts throughout high school. Wayne was a musician and was a tailor by trade. In 1975, two years before I graduated from high school, Wayne moved away to Washington, D.C., to work.

During our separation, I began to develop a more profound yearning to know more about Jesus Christ. I received the baptism of the Holy Spirit in 1976. My Christian life as a young adult became more fulfilling. I mentored and worked with The Singing Angels, a youth singing group in the community. I won an oratorical contest at my high school. I began to recognize my identity as an individual . In 1977, I graduated from high school as part of the first graduating class of South Florence High.

In 1978, Wayne returned from Washington. We rekindled our relationship. Wayne had given his life to Jesus Christ also. I felt that God had sent him back into my life. We prayed and talked about our future together. One weekend he visited me and proposed. I accepted his proposal and we became engaged. On June 9, 1979, I married my high-school sweetheart. Two days later I moved with my husband to Washington, D.C., into a one-bedroom apartment one block away from the subway station.

I was nineteen, a young girl, fragile, and naïve. I feared leaving my home and meeting new people. Adjusting to life in the city was not easy. I experienced the huge change coming from a quiet rural area to the busy, noisy city.

Wayne worked for the Department of Labor, and I worked at a bank. I walked to the subway and the bus stop to get transportation to work and church. I made friends with my husband's friends. I joined The Lighthouse Church, a church filled with loving people. They witnessed and showed the love of God to others. I began to feel at peace about being away from my family in South Carolina. With Jesus Christ, I was experiencing life in a new dimension.

I found the first year of marriage to be a time of adjustment. Wayne and I set goals and expectations for our future. We wanted to buy a house and a car, and we wanted to have children. I felt happy and blessed, and everything around me gave me joy. I was living my dream of living happily-ever after.

One year after being married, I became pregnant. However, early in the first trimester of pregnancy I had a miscarriage. The doctor said there was no apparent reason. A few months later, I became pregnant again. My husband and I were thrilled. I experienced the wonderful joy of pregnancy and the anticipation of giving birth. My husband and I attended the Lamaze childbirth class to prepare for the birth of our child. We waited anxiously, and on April 29, 1981, I gave birth to a 6 1/2 pound healthy baby boy that we named Dwayne.

Having a child transformed our lives. I felt the amazing power of my love for him. I became fulfilled in being a mother. Wayne and I watched the child that I had carried for nine months grow and develop his own characteristics. I loved hearing the sound of his laughter. Whenever he heard my voice, he turned, looking at me with a big smile. Our son continued to develop in his infancy stage. I watched him learn to roll over from his stomach to his back. I would often sit him up and he balanced himself. I held him in my arms, brushing his smooth, silky, black hair, thinking about his future when he would grow up.

To accommodate our growing family, we later moved from the one-bedroom apartment to a two-bedroom apartment. Being a mother gratified my life. We were working parents with a typical routine. The babysitter picked up our son every day, and she would bring him home when we returned home from work. After being married for two years with a seven- month-old son, life seemed content.

On November 25, 1981, I went to work and returned home, just a usual day. On that evening, I played with my son. We played our usual game. I pressed my lips against his belly, and he laughed. Then I placed him on the floor, and to my surprise he crawled a little for the first time. This was exciting. I proudly proclaimed to my husband, "He'll be walking soon!"

After having dinner that evening, I decided to go to church. Wayne stayed at home with the baby. I left home around 7:00 p.m. and I returned around 10:00 p.m. The service at church gave me great joy. I remembered the words of a song the soloist had sung. The words echoed in my spirit: "It has been worth having the Lord in my life--living in a world of darkness, He brought me the light." When I return home that nigh, I walked upstairs to our apartment on the second floor rejoicing in my spirit.

As I turned the doorknob to our apartment, I had no idea what awaited me behind that door. I opened the door turning my head to the right, looking straight into the living room. I saw my son lying on the floor with a trash bag over his face! I ran into the apartment horrified. I reach down and removed the bag and picked up my baby. I picked up his small, limp body. His eyes did not open, and he appeared lifeless. I tried to awaken him, but he did not respond. I yelled, "Dwayne! Dwayne!" I became fearful and confused. I screamed as loudly as I could, "Jesus, help me! Jesus, help me!" I placed my ear against his chest listening for his heartbeat. I held him close to my body praying that his eyes would open.

I then screamed for Wayne. He came running down from his sister's apartment where he had been--leaving our son alone! I yelled, "Call 911." He went to his sister's apartment to use the phone to call for help. When he returned, he took the baby from my arms giving him CPR. I knelt beside my child praying and crying that he would live and not die. I could feel my heart beating fast and began to panic and shook with fear.

The ambulance and the paramedics arrived within a few minutes, but the minutes felt like forever. The paramedics worked on him and said he was still alive. They informed me they were taking him to the nearest hospital. As they rolled him away on the stretcher, I walked behind them, thinking only about my son. My heart continued beating fast, and my legs were getting weak. I cried uncontrollably begging God to save Dwayne's life. I tried to get into the ambulance, but the paramedics said I could not ride along with my child.

Devastated, my husband and I rode in the car following the ambulance. My mind was tormented with thoughts of my baby's condition. Was he going to survive? Please, Lord let this be so!

Arriving at the hospital, I ran frantically into the emergency room. I could not breathe and felt as if I were walking through a thick fog. In spite of my need and deep desire to go directly to be with my baby, they directed us to the registration booth where I nervously gave them the information they required.

Once we were released from the mandatory registration process, we went back into the waiting room as our child fought for his life. My family, pastor, and many of my Christian brothers and sisters came to the hospital to support us in prayer. We sat in a small room separated from the main emergency waiting area. I remember my agony. Thoughts ran rapidly through my mind as I tried to grapple with and understand what happened. I heard conversations going on all around me and could not connect to anything or anyone. I felt myself biting nervously and intently on my bottom lip.

The hours passed as slowly as a turtle's pace. Around 3:00 a.m., the doctors came out to give us the news. I will always remember and have often wished it was just a horrible scene in a nightmare. They simply said, "We did all we could." My hope faded, and the pain of the thought of my baby's lost life led to tears from a broken heart. I knew everyone around felt the same pain as I did because they too were crying tears of sympathy or empathy.

A nurse came into the waiting room and asked if I wanted to see my son. From my haze of tears and confused mind, I answered, "Yes." As I entered the room where he was lying, I looked around and became aware of the machines and tubes the doctors had probably used to try to revive Dwayne, but they were now standing idle after all of man's resources were depleted.

I looked down on my son and touched his beautiful, soft skin. I felt his still, warm skin. My baby looked as if he were sleeping. Such a short time had passed since I had held my living, breathing baby in my arms. My healthy seven-month-old baby boy was dead. I now stood over his dead body never to hear his joyful laughter again. At this point, I mentally shut down.

On that night, I left my son's bedside disconsolate. Before leaving the hospital my husband and I were approached by police investigators. They took us into a small room to question us about the circumstances of our son's death. I felt puzzled and shocked talking to the police. One investigator began to explain that my child's death was under routine investigation. I asked why. He said it was because the incident occurred in our home. They asked us to explain what happened. My husband told them he had gone upstairs. He explained to the investigators that, in that short time, Dwayne had crawled under the sofa and had gotten the trash bags stored there.

I told them I had gone to church, returned home, and upon opening my apartment door, found my son with a trash bag over his face. I told them I screamed, and my husband came running down from his sister's upstairs apartment. They questioned us for about an hour at the hospital and then took us to our apartment to continue their investigation.

I did not want to go back into that apartment. I shivered as I walked up the stairs. Through my tears, I could hear myself repeating over and over, "My baby is dead. My baby is dead." Walking into the living room, I remember screaming because the bag was still on the floor. I showed the investigators where I had found my baby. The investigators walked through the apartment. After what seemed to be an eternity, they ended this tedious and painful ordeal. Before leaving, they said my son's death appeared to have been an accident.

I could not stay in our apartment. My pastor's wife took us to their home. I was an emotional wreck and took medication to calm my nerves. I cried myself to sleep. The next day Elder David Bryan, the pastor's son, took Wayne to the apartment to get us some clothes. When he returned, I saw a cold look in his eyes. My heart filled with pain realizing that we had lost more than our son that night.

Despite our pain and grief, we continued to work on the funeral arrangements. My sister-in-law, Deloris, and others from the church helped with the arrangements. I searched and searched until I could find a white suit for Dwayne's burial. I felt a white suit represented the purity of the angel that God gave me for such a short time.

Wayne could not deal with Dwayne's death. I was unable to comfort him, and as I too could not comprehend my baby's death, Wayne could not comfort me. A wall of pain, anger, and frustration seemed to be building between my husband and me.

The wake was held on that Friday night, November 27, at Stewart's Funeral Home in Washington, D.C. Family, friends, and co-workers attended. The service was beautiful and ended with prayer.

When the service was over, I stood in the foyer of the funeral home looking for my husband. I discovered he had left earlier with one of his friends. I left the service feeling hurt and abandoned. I had to go on alone to complete the program for the next day's funeral service. However, as always, God made a way and placed people in my life to assist. Sister Ann Davis and some others were there to help me complete the task. After completing the arrangements, I went to my husband's brother's home where we were invited to spend the night.

The next day I got up fatigued, mentally and physically, from the unbearable thought that this was the day of my baby's funeral. I muttered to myself that I am only twenty-two and burying my seven-month-old child. It just wasn't right that a child should precede his parents in death.

The funeral service was held at Lighthouse Church in Maryland. My most vivid memory of the service was the final kiss I gave my son, and as I did I remember thanking God that Dwayne had been a happy child for the time he had been in my life.

We had planned for Dwayne's body to be shipped back to our home in Florence, South Carolina, for burial and a graveside service, but the funeral home told us they could not ship the body to our home in Florence, South Carolina. So we had to make other plans. Our alternative was to transport our son's body ourselves. Wayne and his friend, Andy Wilson drove the body to Florence, South Carolina. I couldn't bear the thought of riding down I-95 in the same vehicle with my sweet child's deceased body. I rode in a car with friends following Wayne and Andy.

The ride to South Carolina took almost seven hours. My words were few as we traveled. In my mind, I relived my child's life seeing him laughing and playing and later seeing him dead in a casket. These visions kept playing in my mind as if my mind were on auto replay. After arriving in Florence, South Carolina, they took my son's body to the funeral home. That night we stayed at my mother-in-law's home. Family and friends came by to offer their condolences. The graveside service would be held on the following day.

As we all gathered at the grave site on that cold and windy day, I felt a sense of division between Wayne and me. He stood on one side of the grave, while I stood with my parents on the other side. I appreciated the comfort of my mother's arms, as I wept at the site where my innocent child was being lowered into a cold, isolated grave. But I also needed the assuring embrace of my husband's arms. I was twenty-two years old. This had been the first death of an immediate family member I had ever experienced.

That sense of division I had felt as I stood at our child's graveside became stark reality when Wayne and I returned to our home in Washington, D.C. We walked around our apartment in a cold, unpleasant atmosphere. Our marriage was on a roller-coaster ride. It seemed as if I could not do anything right. I tried to imagine what my husband felt as he tried to deal with our son's death, but I couldn't because I was not yet able to deal with it myself. I spent many dark nights crying myself to sleep. I felt alone and abandoned.

In an attempt to save our marriage, we decided to take a trip. We flew to New York to spend time together away from our place of pain, and hopefully to a place of peace and happiness; but little did we realize that peace and happiness is not a place. Our trip was anything but reconciling. There was just too much unspoken pain and bitterness. After I went to sleep, Wayne left to go out to find his peace and happiness in the New York nightlife, only to return in the early morning. Nothing we had hoped to accomplish on this trip came to be. We seemed further apart than we were before this so- called renewing-our-marriage trip. We returned home with nothing accomplished and more confused than ever.

Back home again and to my dismay, Wayne eventually confessed he no longer loved me. Anger filled my mind as it became more evident that our marriage was in trouble. The man that I married had turned into a stranger. He would not pay the rent and wasted his money. He continued to stay out all night. Our marriage continued to fall apart.

I tried to go on, hoping and praying that God would fix our marriage. I kept my daily routine the best that I could. I went to work every day at the bank, but dreaded going home. I felt empty and hollow within. I had not only buried my son, but it also seemed as if my marriage was buried too.

I battled with low self-esteem. Although I was doing all I could to deal with the grief over the loss of my baby, now my marriage was falling apart. I struggled to hold on to the values I had learned as a young girl.

I did not want to blame my husband wrongfully for my son's death; I had to come to grips as to how my baby died. However, I was beginning to hear rumors and different accounts. I continued on through the rumors, the pain of grief, and the fear of a marriage going wrong. There were many questions left unanswered, questions I had not yet asked. Truthfully, in my mind, I questioned if Wayne killed my child. People were beginning to ask me questions like, "How was it possible for the baby to get to the trash bags?" The only answer I could give was that my child was dead. Within myself I locked away all questions concerning my child's death.

I cried many nights while listening to the radio for comfort because Wayne was not there. One such night, as I listened to a song called "Uncloudy Day," I prayed for an "uncloudy" day. During this season of sorrow, God comforted me through this verse: "For his anger endureth but a moment; in his favour is life: weeping may endure for a night, but joy cometh in the morning" (Psalm 30:5).

I asked Jesus, “When would this morning arrive?” Jesus’ answer that my morning would arrive when I could see Him in the midst of my tests and trials.

The Choices

Be not far from me; for trouble is near;
for there is none to help.
Psalm 22:11

One year after our son's death, I reached a pivotal point in my life. Wayne and I finally came to terms with the fact that we could no longer stay together. I left my husband and moved in with Alice, a sister and a friend in Christ. After separating, Wayne and I still attended the same church. However, Wayne left the church six months later. I stayed with Alice for about one year, and then I got my own apartment.

I prayed sincerely for my heart to be emptied of bitterness and an unforgiving spirit. Almost two years after our separation in January of 1984, Wayne and I tried to reconcile, and I became pregnant. However, Wayne left and moved to New Orleans. I soon felt the inner wounds of rejection from being pregnant and abandoned. My heart was broken and my life in shambles. The only explanation my husband gave for moving to New Orleans was that he wanted to follow his career as a designer. I had opened my heart to love him again, and he walked out. What an unexpected blow! Many nights I cried and pressed my face into the pillow calling myself stupid and dumb. How could I make such a mistake? I gave love and it was denied. The little girl inside of me was seeking love and acceptance.

Despite the pain of Wayne's rejection and betrayal, nine months passed by and the due date of the birth of my baby grew near. Wayne began to call from New Orleans and said he wanted to be in his child's life. I told him "I do not need you." Wayne was making plans to move back to

Washington, D. C., and he arrived a few months before my baby's birth.

On October 25, 1984, I went into labor. When I got to the hospital, the doctor said the baby was in distress. The doctor did an emergency caesarean-section delivery. They called my husband, and he came to the hospital. I said to my girlfriend, Yolanda "I do not want to see him." I later decided to let him come in.

My baby boy survived the delivery weighing 6½ pounds. They placed the baby on my chest. The doctor asked what his name was and I answered, "Justin." Someone said, "A good name, he came just in time." I brought my son home from the hospital and stayed on leave for three months.

I struggled financially to support my child and me. Wayne came over several times to see the baby. However, I felt our marriage was over, and I wanted to go on with my life. I struggled to stay in my apartment. The months passed and the financial burden of raising a child alone became too much.

James and Shirley, my son's godparents, invited me to stay in their home. They said I did not have to pay rent, just save my money. After saving enough money, I moved to Virginia Beach. I worked and provided for my son hoping to start my life over. However, my son began to experience developmental problems. I dealt with the struggles of single parenthood and raising my son. I had to work and take my son to physical therapy three times a week.

Wayne remained in Washington, D.C. On November 6, 1985, I received an unexpected call. I heard my phone ringing and when I answered "hello," Wayne said, "Hi, how are you?" I responded "fine," but my heart immediately dropped, and I felt an emotional feeling of unrest. He said he was calling to ask me to forgive him, and that he wanted his family back. He said he had repented and had rededicated his life to Christ. However, as usual, I heard no feeling or emotions behind his words. He said he knew that God could restore our marriage. My mind overwhelmed by the thought of us reconciling. I quickly ended the call and said I did not want to talk about it.

Wayne continued calling and continued to ask me to seek God's guidance. He said he knew God wanted us to reconcile. He gave me the phone number of his pastor and the church he was attending. I prayed, I talked to his pastor, my pastor, and to friends and family in an attempt to seek counsel and guidance. I finally resolved that the choice was mine and prayed that God would help me make the right decision. I wrestled with the thought of reconciling with my husband, and I wanted my motives to be right. I questioned myself repeatedly and became perplexed wondering if I should reconcile and give our marriage another chance? It became a choice between struggling with separation and giving up on a seemingly hopeless marriage, or trusting in God's power to heal and restore our marriage.

My thoughts deepened as I reviewed my Christian obligation to give our marriage a try. I began to think about my life and how blessed I was with both parents in my life. I felt within myself that my son deserved the same. With love in my heart for Christ, I wanted to do what was right in His sight, knowing that God desired that families be restored. I finally agreed with Wayne, and we proceeded toward reconciliation.

We began to make plans to reconcile. Wayne came to Virginia Beach and brought Justin and me back with him to Washington, D.C., where we reunited as a family on April 4, 1986. I prayed, asking God to give me a new heart to love my husband. I asked God to work in my life to fulfill His purpose and plan. I felt confident that God was at work, just as He promises in Philippians 1:6: "Being confident of this very thing, that he which hath begun a good work in you will perform it until the day of Jesus Christ."

Shortly after returning to Washington D.C. I began to work at The American Youth Hostels as an accounting assistant. Later Wayne and I both became employees at the U.S. Department of Labor. We purchased our first home on June 3, 1987. I recall Wayne saying "I thank God for restoring our marriage" and that these were the best years of his life. We both experienced the awesome power of God reconciling and transforming our marriage from the dead.

Wayne was a tailor by trade and he began to reach new heights in his profession. They featured him on television on The Cathy Hughes show and in the Washington Post newspaper. They sold his clothes in one of the finest boutiques in Georgetown, Washington, D.C. He designed and tailored wardrobes for many of his customers.

I experienced the awesome power of Jesus Christ resurrecting our marriage from the grave. Through Jesus Christ, I could love my husband again. Christ became the head of our home as we worshipped and prayed together. Many of the problems of the past vanished.

My World Turned Upside Down

∞∞∞

Hear my cry, O God; attend unto my prayer. From the end of the earth will I cry unto thee, when my heart is overwhelmed: lead me to the rock that is higher than I.
PSALM 61:1-2

In the summer of 1987, after moving into our new home, an unexpected trial came into our lives. One day I went out to lunch with my best friend, Yolanda. In the midst of our conversation, I found myself saying, "I do not think Wayne will be with me long." Those words just came out of my mouth, although I didn't understand what they meant. I could not overcome this feeling, and I later realized I was sensing the tragedy ahead.

I had had many trials before this one, but nothing but the grace of God took me through the trial that lay ahead. My husband started having physical problems and could not sleep or eat. I took him to one doctor, and he could not find out what was wrong. I took him to another doctor, and he suggested Wayne take the AIDS test.

One day while I was at work, Wayne called to tell me the test results. I can still remember him saying "The AIDS test came back positive!" I had no response to those words. Chills ran through my body, and I hung up the phone and burst into tears. I ran to the bathroom so no one could see me crying. One of my Korean coworkers asked, "Are you alright?" I answered that I didn't feel well and that I had to go home.

My emotions overwhelmed me and I left work, walking in the rain to the bus stop. I rode the bus in anguish and struggled hard to keep the tears back. I got off the bus and walked to my home. I walked up on my front porch, wet from the rain and filled with pain. Wayne opened the door and asked if I was okay. I stood in the foyer of my doorway crying, then walked into our home feeling empty and angry. My happy home that had been filled with peace, joy, and love became filled with fear and confusion.

I wrestled with my thoughts and fears. I could not imagine being HIV positive. We finally decided to see a specialist in infectious diseases who could test us. At an area hospital, in the infectious disease department, they tested my husband again, and I took my first HIV test. A week later, the doctor called to schedule an appointment to give us the test results.

On a very beautiful day in the summer of 1987, I walked into the doctor's office and received news that nearly drove me insane. I sat down and watched as the doctor opened our files then listened as he announced the test results: "I am afraid I have bad news. Your test came back, and you are both HIV positive." I wrapped my arms around myself. Wayne did not say a word. The doctors said that Wayne's T cell counts were almost depleted and his immune system had been compromised. I sat there as the doctor accused him of knowing that he had the virus before now. He prescribed Wayne the drug AZT, a drug used to delay development of AIDS (acquired immunodeficiency syndrome). He said that my T count was high and did not put me on medication. He said that unfortunately I probably was recently infected because my cell counts were almost normal. The doctor told us to make a follow-up appointment. He gave us brochures on HIV. I quickly placed them in my purse. After hearing the test results, it appeared the whole world stood still. In one day everything changed, after discovering my husband and I had the AIDS virus.

We took a cab home. I gazed out the window not talking to my husband. When I arrived home, I went into my basement without turning on the light, and I sat in my dark basement with the blinds pulled down. A few hours later Wayne came down. I told him to "Forget me," that my life was over; and I said, "you knew you had the virus and did not tell me." I told him to "leave me alone," and that my sole concern was about who would care for my son, Justin if I died. My main reason for reconciling was to give my son a father, and now it appeared that AIDS would take both of us from him.

I stayed in that dark basement, crying, consumed with grief for days. I had never experienced such pain; I had had other pains, but this surpassed them all. I felt betrayed, hurt, angry, ashamed, and humiliated; but the most miserable feeling of all was that I could not feel the presence of God. All these emotions compressed into one pain that I could not possibly describe. I thought I was going insane. It was all consuming as if nothing existed outside this horrible inner wound of my heart.

My mind became filled with horrifying questions. How did my husband get AIDS? Was he a homosexual? Did he use drugs? Did he come back to me to cover his sins, hoping God would heal him if he did the right thing? My mind filled with so many questions. I confronted my husband with my questions. He told me he did not know how he got AIDS, and he said he was not a homosexual. I felt naïve thinking no one would knowingly hurt another. I became devastated, thinking my life was over. How could I ever trust anyone again? Why would he do this to me? I hated him for putting my life through this turmoil. I was a twenty-seven- year-old woman feeling as if I was sitting in hell with unending torment.

My heart was consumed in utter turmoil from Friday afternoon until Monday morning. I came up periodically to look out the kitchen window onto the deck of my home. I went from the basement to the upstairs bedroom and looked out my bedroom window. The world outside looked dead. I had no words for my husband. I went back to the basement and cried out to God for understanding. My husband came down to the basement asking, "Are you going to leave me? You have every right to leave." I looked at him with horror. My greatest pain was that he never showed any emotion, and all the time my emotions were tearing me apart. I bathed myself in my own tears.

During that hard time, my mind was flooded with a range of emotions. I have chosen to share openly the emotions and turmoil that raged within me during that time, because I promised the Lord that I would open the windows of my soul and share my life to give Him glory.

Anger

My first response was anger. Anger raged within me against my husband and against God. I felt God had let me down. I could not understand how this could happen to me, and I asked God why. I reminded Him that I did what I thought would please Him. I then started pointing fingers at others that I tried to blame for what had happened. However, I directed the greatest anger against myself. The words "you do not know God" resounded in my mind as mockery. I felt angry about being dull in my spirit in understanding God's leading and for trusting my emotions. That is why I write this book so openly, not to expose or blame anyone, but as an admonition to others to seek God's wisdom when looking for direction in their lives.

Guilt

Following the turmoil of anger, guilt overcame me. Guilt came knocking and guilt spoke to my mind saying, "This is your sentence. If you had stayed with your husband, he never would have gotten AIDS." No one can escape such a charge, except through the grace, peace, and the presence of Almighty God. Through the blood of Jesus, I overcame this condemnation from the enemy that sought to destroy me, and I found rest in Romans 8:28: "And we know that all things work together for good to them that love God, to them who are the called according to his purpose."

Humiliation and Shame

For a while, I allowed humiliation and shame to become my clothing. Humiliated beyond words, the enemy of my soul tore me apart with vicious fantasies of my dishonor. The devil filled my mind with thoughts of what a failure I was. I did not have the strength to cast down those imaginations that were contrary to the Word of God, although we are admonished by Scripture to do that: "Casting down imaginations, and every high thing that exalteth itself against the knowledge of God, and bringing into captivity every thought to the obedience of Christ" (2 Cor. 10:5).

I was in a fight and my opponent, the devil, was not fighting fair. He enjoyed hitting me with every vile accusation when I was down, and I agreed with my enemy the devil. I came to Jesus, just as I was, weary, beaten down, and oppressed. I did not want bitter emotions to control me.

I was alone and isolated. I cut off many ties to friendships from the past, yet the loneliness I suffered as a consequence made me feel neglected and forgotten. I offered my loneliness to God. During this time I often read the words on a plaque that was on my wall at work: "...Yea, they may forget, yet will I not forget thee (Isaiah 49:15). Behold, I have graven thee upon the palms of my hands; ..." (Isaiah 49:16).

The Way Out

∞∞∞

There hath no temptation taken you but such as is common to man: but God is faithful, who will not suffer you to be tempted above that ye are able; but will with the temptation also make a way to escape, that ye may be able to bear it.
1 Corinthians 10:13

Acceptance

I accepted the facts and decided to walk in the truth of God's word. He said He would never leave us nor forsake us. I did not want to go down this road without Christ. I purposed in my heart to do whatever I could, so that together, Wayne and I could serve the Lord.

Forgiveness

I prayed, seeking the way to forgive. I asked the Lord to show me how to forgive Wayne. It became hard because Wayne showed little emotion about our desperate circumstances. One day when I was on my knees praying and crying, God gave me a revelation of forgiveness. God brought to mind a Sunday school class from years before. In my mind my teacher, Mother Watson, was teaching about forgiveness. She taught that we could not base forgiveness on our feelings, but that Jesus commands us to forgive despite our emotions. Mark 11:26 came to mind: "But if ye do not forgive, neither will your Father which is in heaven forgive your trespasses."

I told the Lord I would forgive, admitting to Him that I couldn't possibly do it without His supernatural help. On that day, I received revelation on forgiveness, and I chose to walk in forgiveness toward the one who had wronged me.

I went to Wayne and said, "Wayne, I will forgive you, and I will stay with you." God miraculously took the torture of an unforgiving spirit, anger, and guilt from my heart. That step of forgiveness was the first footprint of a miracle walk with Christ. Through forgiveness, I received God's grace that released me from internal destruction. I will not pretend that after choosing to forgive it was easy. It was not. I had to fight the enemy of my soul every step of the way to walk in love and stick to the decision to stay by Wayne's side. I asked God to love through me.

A Miraculous Walk in Agape Love

After the decision to forgive and to stay with my husband, God gave me the ability to walk in *agape* love. This love is stronger than any other love. This love allowed me to love the one who had wronged me. *Agape* love became a miracle footprint in my life, and this love gave me the strength to stay with my husband. This is the love that is described in 1 Cor. 13:4-6: "Love is patient, love is kind. It does not envy, it does not boast, it is not proud. It is not rude, it is not self-seeking, it is not easily angered, it keeps no record of wrongs. Love does not delight in evil but rejoices with the truth" (NIV).

When the Holy Spirit brings this *agape* love, it strips you of yourself. I couldn't explain to others my motives or my decision. I forgave Wayne and chose to stay with him. The power and love of God upheld our marriage. Through the grace of God, I could love in sickness and in health as I had promised in my wedding vows. As a result, I found myself walking on a path I call "footprints of a miracle"--a walk that has revealed God to me as Jehovah-Shalom--"The Lord is my peace." And surely "the Lord is my peace." Jehovah-

Shalom has been ever present in my life. Judges 6:24 comes to mind: "Then Gideon built an altar there unto the Lord, and called it Jehovah-Shalom."

I believe Wayne lived as long as he did because of my decision to walk in love and forgiveness despite the attacks of the enemy. I stayed with Wayne, and our fight with AIDS began.

The Lonely Dark Trail

∞∞∞

Though I walk in the midst of trouble, thou wilt revive me.
Psalm 138:7

When we found out that we were HIV positive, my husband asked me not to tell anyone. However, as time passed I chose to tell his immediate family because I knew I would need their help in caring for him. His mother told me it was my responsibility as his wife and that they would help me. I felt healthy and therefore committed myself to take care of my husband. I did not focus on my diagnosis of having the HIV virus.

Wayne was the youngest boy in a family of nine. Wayne's mother, brothers, and sisters helped in giving him quality care and doing all they could to contribute to the quality of his life. They helped me tremendously in caring for him and supported him without reservation. His family loved him unconditionally. His mother and three of his sisters lived in another state. However, they visited him often. He had three sisters who lived in the area that helped in his care. His sister Gwen was always willing to keep our son when I stayed with Wayne overnight in the hospital.

The doctor gave Wayne the diagnosis of full-blown AIDS in 1987, after he had stayed in the hospital for two weeks. They discovered that he had kidney problems. They said his kidneys would eventually fail, and that he would go on dialysis.

While Wayne was in the hospital, I became aware of

the stigma and harsh treatment attached to those having AIDS. The hospital care was cruel and without compassion. I compared my husband's treatment with how a leper was treated in the Bible: "He shall remain unclean all the days during which he has the infection; he is unclean. He shall live alone; his dwelling shall be outside the camp" (Lev. 13:46 NASB).

I did not dare leave Wayne alone. I asked for a cot, so I could sleep by his bed. I never left my husband's side at night. His family and I had to bathe him ourselves.

There were warning signs outside the door. The staff that picked up the food trays wore gloves. They did not clean his room until his family and I reported it to the administration. Everyone was afraid. I understood their fears, but I loved Wayne and suffered because I understood that these AIDS patients were people with feelings too.

In the morning, after being at the hospital all night long, I went to work. Some days on my lunch hour I would take the bus to visit him and then go back to work. Later, I would go home to get clean clothes and return to the hospital to stay by his bedside. I sat by his bed listening to religious tapes and reading my Bible. People would come in and look at me in confusion.

One day a nurse came in and saw me reading my Bible. She took me outside the door and said: "Do you know what is wrong with your husband?" I said, "Yes." She then asked how I could possibly stay with him. I told her that God forgives this sin just like any other, and that I had no choice but to forgive.

After that two-week stay in the hospital, Wayne came home. The doctors said he could no longer work. The doctors filled out the disability forms. However, Wayne's appetite and strength returned, so he decided to go back to work. The doctors monitored his kidneys. Wayne's health remained stable for over one year.

As the year passed, I watched God soften Wayne's heart. I would find him crying many nights. He told me he was grateful that I did not leave him. I felt peace in my heart to be living beyond myself and to sense the power of Jesus Christ within me.

Almost two years after Wayne's diagnosis of full blown AIDS, on January 20, 1989, Wayne entered the hospital because his kidneys had failed. They started him on the dialysis machine. The doctors said he would be in the hospital for about one week. Wayne stayed in the hospital from January 20 through February 23, 1989, because of medical complications.

On February 1, 1989, we celebrated Wayne's thirty-third birthday in the hospital. The doctor said he was doing well, and they would be releasing him soon. We were happy. However, two weeks later I started noticing a change in Wayne's health. He started having high fevers, kept repeating himself, and started having delusions. He would tell me repeatedly to go home because he was coming home soon.

One night Wayne leaped over the bed rails, pulled out all of his tubes, and put on his coat to go home. Another time, he got up in the middle of the night and walked into the wall, saying it was time to go with his brother and father, both of whom had already died. After walking into the wall he said, "I guess it is not time to go yet," and he got back into bed. His health continued to decline.

While at the hospital with my husband, I walked up and down the halls. I saw many other patients with AIDS. I saw people dying who had no desire for God. I saw gay men crying because their lovers had passed away. I knew

God hated this sin of homosexuality, but I also knew that He loved the people. I watched with sadness and with the desire to tell them about the love of God.

God gave me an opportunity to talk with a woman with AIDS in the room next to my husband's room. I went into her room. She told me she was homeless and had gotten the virus through drugs. I began to think that I would one day be like this woman. I started to feel the pain for myself and her. I asked her if I could pray for her and she agreed. I held her hands and prayed for her. After praying, I hugged her and gave her a Bible to read. A week later, she was not in that room. I wondered if she had died or had been released from the hospital. However, I was glad that I had told her about Jesus Christ.

I continued my ordeal and my routine of staying with my husband. I began to realize that the AIDS virus has touched many people's lives. I saw people losing their love ones, friends, and acquaintances to this terrible disease. I saw different races and genders. This acquired immunodeficiency syndrome (AIDS) is not a single, distinct disease but rather a disorder characterized by severe suppression of the immune system. The immunodeficiency renders the body susceptible to a variety of normally manageable infections, cancers, and other diseases.

Wayne's health continued to decline until he became comatose. I continued to stay by his bed reading the Bible to him. He responded with groaning. I knew his spirit was receiving the Word of God even though he could not talk. He would respond when I read from Psalm 103: "Bless the Lord, O my soul: and all that is within me, bless his holy name. Bless the Lord, O my soul, and forget not all his benefits: who forgiveth all thine iniquities; who healeth all thy diseases; who redeemeth thy life from destruction; who crowneth thee with loving kindness and tender mercies" (Psalm 103:1-4).

I tried not to call on the medical staff to help me very much. However, one day Wayne was lifeless, and I could not turn him myself. I called the medical staff, and they did not respond to my call. I pressed the intercom again crying, "Please come and help me." I began to feel the pressure of caring for him.

Wayne's condition continued to worsen. I talked to doctors, and they said he needed a blood transfusion. I sat in his room for two days waiting for them to give him blood. Two days passed, and he had not gotten the blood transfusion.

On Monday, February 20, 1989, I called the doctor's office from the hospital to ask about the transfusion. The doctor asked if anyone was with me. When I answered no, he said tests showed that the infection had entered Wayne's brain. He said, "I am afraid your husband is dying, and we have done all we can." He said they were making sure that he was in no pain. I hung up the phone. I went out of the room, because I did not want Wayne to hear me crying. I sat on the floor outside his door with my head between my legs weeping and crying. I later called my job and told them my husband was dying, and I did not know when I would return to work. I stayed by his bedside. His family and others came to visit. However, I kept visitations to a limit.

On Thursday, February 23, 1989, a nurse came into his room, held my hand, and said: "I'll be praying for you today." My spirit immediately felt the urgency to call his family to come to the hospital. I began to feel in my spirit that death was going to destroy all my hopes for his recovery. Later that morning I went to the lobby to make some calls. I called my best friend, Yolanda, and told her the doctors did not think he would make it. She asked me if I wanted her to come to the hospital, and I told her no. However, as a true friend, she heard beyond my words and came. I also called my sister-in-law Deloris, cried, and told her about my pain. Deloris said, "The Lord said to let him go." I told her I couldn't, but then I finally said, "I'll let him go." She prayed with me. I returned to his room, knowing in my heart, he was dying. I walked into his room and felt a cold shiver, feeling knowing that death was near. Shortly after that, my friend Yolanda walked in and touched him as he took his last, final deep breath of life. The doctor came in and pronounced Wayne dead at 11:45 a.m. My only thought was that I had let him go. I saw the peaceful look on his face. His sister Patricia walked in and asked if Wayne was asleep. I replied, "No Pat, he has died."

Immediately after Wayne's death, the hospital officials took the family to a conference room. Everyone was crying except me. I had no tears left. I was only angry and bitter. Wayne had promised he would never leave me. I felt abandoned. The first second after Wayne took his last breath, many of those fears that I had given to God after learning he had the AIDS virus returned. The pandemonium of anger and unforgiving thoughts resurfaced. Sitting in that conference room, I experienced the fear of living and the fear of dying. I knew I had to get myself together and deal with his death. I sat with his brothers and sisters as we discussed which funeral home would get his body. I decided to use the same funeral home I had used seven years ago for my son Dwayne. While we were talking, they came to escort us back into the room where his body lay. A few minutes later his doctor came in and sat in the chair across from my dead husband. He looked over at me and said in a very sincere voice, "You do not have to die this way you know."

I struggled wondering how I would survive. I was consumed with anger and grief. I saw no direction and no hope. The focus of my life had changed abruptly, and my concerns were now for me and my son. I looked fearfully at the road ahead being a thirty-year-old widow with a four-year-old son.

I left my dead husband's bedside and walked down the halls looking into every room that I passed, and then spoke with the hospital administration about having Wayne's body released to Stewart Funeral Home. As I proceeded to leave the hospital, I suddenly remembered that this day was the scheduled date of closing for the refinancing of our home. We had started the refinancing process before Wayne went into the hospital. The settlement date was scheduled for February 23, at 3:00 p.m. I was taken aback thinking, my husband died at 11:45 a.m., three hours and fifteen minutes before the scheduled closing appointment. I began to think about what I should do. I decided to keep the appointment. In distress, I asked my friend Yolanda to drive me to the lawyer's office. As Yolanda drove our car, the car my husband used to drive himself to the hospital, I began to pound my fist in fury on the dashboard screaming, "Why God, why?"

I walked into the lawyer's office in a daze and told the lawyer that my husband had died that day. I began crying and told them I did not know what to do. The receptionist gave me a cup of water to drink to help calm my nerves. My girlfriend Yolanda stood by my side to comfort me. Meanwhile, the lawyer quickly went into his office. Later, he returned and said he made some calls to determine how to handle the matter. He showed compassion and sympathy recommending that I refinance because the house payments would be lower. I signed the refinancing papers.

Still, in a daze I went to where the immediate family had gathered at my sister-in-law Gwen's home. I remember running to my son crying, hugging, and holding him close. I stayed there for a few hours while Wayne's family and I proceeded to make the funeral arrangements. Later that evening, Wayne's mother left on the 8:00 p.m. train to go to our hometown in Florence, South Carolina, to arrange the service there. My mother and my sister arrived on the 8:00 p.m. train to help me with the arrangements for the service in Washington, D.C. After picking up my mother and sister from the train station, we went home. To my surprise two of my dear friends, Betty and Bernadette, had already removed all Wayne's medicine and cleaned my home, making it tolerable for me to go back into my home.

The next three days involved the heart-wrenching task of planning my husband's funeral. Many friends and family offered support and condolences. I planned to have a memorial service in Washington, D.C., and a funeral service in our hometown of Florence, South Carolina.

On the night of the memorial service in Washington, D.C., I felt tired and worn. I walked into the funeral home holding my son's hand. I did not look to the left or the right. When I approached the casket my heart dropped. I stood over Wayne's body feeling the pain of grief. I went to sit down and my son got up and went back to the casket. I became upset because he wanted to stay by the casket. A family member went to get my son to keep him from standing by the casket.

The service began and Elder William Covington of Greater Lighthouse Church voluntarily took charge of the service. The service gave me comfort through the songs and words of encouragement. Despite the grief, I was able to lift my hands in praise to God.

The next day the funeral home shipped Wayne's body on an Amtrak train to Florence, South Carolina. I took the same train with two of his sisters and two of my closest friends, Yolanda and Betty. When I arrived in my hometown, I walked off the train. While walking into the station, I turned and saw them removing Wayne's body from stowage. In those moments, I felt a deep sense of finality in the realization that our life together had ended. We held his funeral at the church where Wayne's mother was a member. Wayne was buried in our hometown. I stayed there for a few weeks, and then my mother and I returned to Washington.

I was now a lost and frightened young widow with a young child. And I now had to face my own battle with the AIDS virus. Many kind coworkers donated almost 200 hours of leave time. I took time off and later returned to work. However, the change was not easy; I fought to go on. I was having difficulty sleeping in my home. I took sleeping pills. My weight went from 130 to100 pounds. My dress size went from a size nine to a size four.

I experienced the pain of grief, but right in the middle of the pain, I had peace--peace because I hadn't walked away. I had loved him to the end. I found comfort in the memory of the night when Wayne came out of his semi-comatose state, looked at me and said, "You are the most beautiful person I have ever known." He added that he was sorry he hadn't been a good husband, and added, "Take care of my son and find someone that will be good to you." I believe he saw God's love in me. I felt peace because he was thinking about how my life would go on after his death.

When Wayne died, I did not reveal that he had died from AIDS. Whenever I was asked, I told people the secondary cause of his death, which was cytomegalovirus, known as CMV. CMV is a cluster of viruses causing many diseases, which had spread throughout Wayne's brain and body. I also told people that he had kidney failure. Wayne's dying of AIDS became a horrible, dark secret. Before Wayne's death his family (mother, brother and sisters), and two dear friends, Yolanda and her husband Israel were the only ones who knew about the situation.

The fact that I was HIV positive was also a horrible, dark secret. I was selective about whom I would tell about my condition. I lived carrying the secret of being HIV positive. I encountered the fear among Christians about how to deal with persons with AIDS.

One day I sat in a missionary meeting at my church with some Christians and listened as they talked about AIDS. They talked about how the doctors did not know much about this disease. They talked about how they should deal with people with AIDS. They didn't know that I was HIV positive. I saw people with AIDS being treated as outcasts. I heard preachers on the radio proclaiming AIDS as a punishment. People with AIDS were indeed being treated as the leper in the bible: "And there came a leper to him, beseeching him, and kneeling down to him, and saying unto him, If thou wilt, thou canst make me clean. And Jesus, moved with compassion, put forth his hand, and touched him, and saith unto him, I will; be thou clean (Mark 1:40-41). Jesus freely ministered life and hope to the lepers when everyone else had abandoned them.

The road I traveled was dark and lonely; and I felt, inwardly, as the leper felt who was left outside the gate--alone.

The Road to Recovery

∞∞∞

Restore unto me the joy of thy salvation;
and uphold me with thy free spirit.
Psalm 51:12

I sought to be discreet in terms of the people I would tell about my HIV status. I was told to prepare for death, but I wanted to live. A few months after my husband's death, I decided to confess my condition to others. One Sunday I sat in church seeking comfort and strength. After the service I found myself confessing my condition to my sister-in-law, Deloris. She wrapped her arms around me and led me to the altar for prayer.

Another situation was when I tried to tell my friend Betty. One day I asked her what she would do if she knew someone who had the AIDS virus. She said it wouldn't matter and quickly changed the subject.

At this point, only a few months had passed since I had buried my husband. My mother and father wanted me to move back home to South Carolina. However, my mother and father and my brothers and sisters did not know I was HIV positive. I did not want to be a burden to them, so I stayed in Washington, D.C., and gave my life to God. I knew I needed to change--that I needed to learn how to depend on God and His power to change me from within.

I lived the next six months desiring change. I chose to stop taking sleeping pills and found myself sleeping in the peace of Jesus Christ. The pain of grief was gradually being removed from my heart. Little by little I grew from within. One Tuesday night at prayer service, while at the altar crying and asking God to help me, Yolanda, my best friend whispered in my ear, "Stop praying for yourself and pray for others." I began to pray for others and God turned my eyes from myself to Him.

Through the power of God my focus was being changed. One day when I came home from work, wretchedness gripped my heart. I ran in and shut the door and threw my purse on the chair. I laid myself out flat on my hardwood floor and prayed for God to heal my pain. God spoke to my spirit, saying, "Stop crying and present my Word back to me." He then spoke to me saying, "I am the way, the truth and the life," reflecting this scripture: *"Jesus saith unto him, I am the way, the truth, and the life: no man cometh unto the Father, but by me (John 14:6*). He then told me I needed to know Him in the fellowship of His suffering so I could rise in his resurrection power, reflecting this scripture: *"That I may know him, and the power of his resurrection, and the fellowship of his sufferings, being made conformable unto his death (Phil.3:10).* On that day, I began the search to get to know Jesus Christ in a more excellent way. His life inside of me would lead the way so that His truth would produce a life of peace and power.

I unmasked myself before God, realizing that what I needed was in God. Over time I sensed a change from within, in terms of dealing with the pain and grief in my heart. I asked God to empower my life that I might survive. I knew I could survive this battle with AIDS. I started buying books which proved to be of great assistance in surviving the battle that was before me.

I attended Kenneth Hagin's camp meeting in July 1989 in Tulsa, Oklahoma, where thousands of people gathered to worship God. I went to the camp meeting five months after my husband's death. I nourished my soul on the Word of God. I bought many books and tapes on healing to keep my "inner man" strengthened. I knew many did not understand what I was doing, but I didn't care, because I was fighting for my life. In my battle for my life, I fell more in love with God, and the agony of grief finally left me. All I had left were memories of a man, my husband Wayne, turning from sin and returning to Christ. I was experiencing the awesome power of the love of God that sustained me in my time of need. The pieces of my life were beginning to come back together. I had renewed hope in my heart.

When I returned from the camp meeting, God continued to minister revelation to my spirit. One Sunday afternoon Annie Boyd brought a message that planted a seed of faith in my heart. She took her text from Jeremiah 29:11, "For I know the thoughts that I think toward you, saith the Lord, thoughts of peace and not of evil, to give you an expected end."

This message confirmed God's desires for me and gave me a sense of anticipation. When Annie ministered that message, the Holy Spirit penetrated my spirit. After that message, I knew God had a plan and a purpose for my life. His plans were for good and not for evil. He had planned for me to live and not to die.

A few months later an incident showed the reality of God's plan and protection for my life. One night as my son and I slept, a burglar broke into my home. Downstairs they took a microwave, a TV, and a stereo. They came upstairs where we were sleeping and took my son's video game and his television. They even took the time to steal the small amount of money I had in my purse. My son and I slept through it all, but I awakened as I heard the burglars leaving and shutting the door. I immediately called the police. They took fingerprints and a police report. The burglars were never caught. I was ever so grateful that they did not harm us. The Lord quickly brought to mind Annie Boyd's message and Jeremiah 29:11: "For I know the thoughts that I think toward you, saith the LORD, thoughts of peace, and not of evil, to give you an expected end." I only imagined what may have happened if we had awakened. I praised God for His blood that had covered us that night. I believed that God protected and covered us while my son and I slept soundly. From that day forward, Jeremiah 29:11 has become a scriptural tool of reinforcement for me to use against Satan. Knowing that God has a plan for my life inspires me and gives me hope.

A New Beginning

∞∞∞

And I will restore to you the years that the locust hath eaten, the cankerworm, and the caterpillar, and the palmerworm, my great army which I sent among you
Joel 2:25

One day it happened. I looked, and there were no more tears to shed. My state of helplessness changed to courage. I deeply yearned to serve others and began to do that. One year after the death of my husband, I found myself gradually emerging from the ashes of grief and sorrow. The flame of the Holy Spirit stirred the ashes of my broken heart. I began to feel a spark of hope within, and I saw life differently through the spiritual eyes of hope.

I began to give myself totally to the things of God. I was a missionary, and I worked with the nursing home ministry. I was involved with a prayer group and with women's ministry. In all this, I experienced personal contentment, courage, and inspiration in serving God and others. I began to focus on the mission instead of the pain of my past. Jesus Christ gave my life new direction as He removed the spirit of grief and sorrow and restored joy to my life.

My son Justin was six-years old and attended first grade at a Christian school. He was curious, energetic, and very playful. He was always discovering how things work. He was always on the move and had a limited attention span. I knew I had to rise above my situation, because my son needed me. Therefore, Justin became my motivation, and I chose to rise above my kaleidoscopic prism of despair. Many times my son saw me crying and would go and get a tissue to dry the tears from my eyes.

As time passed, something unexpected happened. The words that Wayne uttered on his deathbed, "Find someone who will be good to you," came to pass. I did not seek out this person, yet someone entered my life who added new purpose, and his name was Samuel. Samuel and I attended the same church, and I became acquainted with him through my best friend Yolanda and her husband Israel. Samuel was Israel's brother, and Israel had been a friend of my deceased husband, Wayne. Through our times of talking and sharing, a unique friendship developed between Samuel and me. Our lives were brought together by the testimonies that we shared.

Samuel had encountered times of hardship and pain throughout his life. He had been in prison. As we began to pray together, Samuel shared with me the pains of his past. I told him that our lives were similar in many ways. Although I had never been in prison as he had, the power of God had released me from my own internal prison of despair. We were two people whose lives and dreams had been broken by life's circumstances.

Through Jesus Christ, I had lived beyond my sorrow and was delivered from the pain of grief. I confessed Jesus Christ as my healer. However, I had no intentions of loving again. Samuel and I became good friends.

One day as we sat together, our conversation took an unexpected turn. "God spoke to my spirit," Samuel shared, "and told me that you would be my wife." I gave a heavy sigh and looked at him in disbelief, thinking to myself--*this man must be crazy.*

I decided to reveal my HIV status to Samuel, so he could move on. I wanted him to understand why I rejected the idea of marriage. Shortly after he shared his thoughts about marriage with me, Samuel and I were sitting in the car talking. "Samuel," I blurted out quickly, "I am HIV positive: Wayne gave me the AIDS virus." Before he could say anything I went on talking..."I don't want to hurt you, but you have the wrong impression about our friendship. I am not looking for a relationship, and I can never have a relationship." I took a deep breath gripping both hands on the steering wheel with my head hung down.

To my dismay, Samuel reached out and grabbed my hand. "I know," he said, "but God said you are to be my wife, and that your sickness is not unto death...God spoke to me, and I want to obey Him." My heart filled with pain as I looked into his eyes. Yet, despite the calm and serene look I saw on Samuel's face, I was not convinced, and my answer was no. While I unequivocally believed Christ to be my Healer, I questioned whether I had the right to put that same burden on someone else. Sitting together that day I held to my viewpoint on not seeking a relationship. And interestingly, Samuel held to his viewpoint as well, simply saying, "Love conquers all, my love...and God's love.

A few months later I sat on my front porch elated as I thought of Jesus Christ. I began to praise and thank Him for saving and keeping me. In the midst of my praise, He spoke to my heart and said I want to do more, but you are putting limits on what I want to do in your life. On that day, I received the confirmation that God brought Samuel and me together for His glory. We went to our pastor for counseling and prayer, and we walked in obedience to Christ.

Six months before our wedding date Samuel and I

joyfully planned our wedding. I married Samuel On December 5, 1992, two years after the death of my first husband. Our marriage ceremony celebrated God's faithfulness and the love we shared. The church was filled with our family, friends, and coworkers.

A highlight of our wedding was when Samuel sang the song "Flesh of my Flesh" to me. My heart filled with joy and love as Samuel began to sing "You are flesh of my flesh and bone of my bones." Tears flowed down my face when he proclaimed in song, "The winds may blow but they won't knock us down. We will stand the test of time because we are standing on holy ground."

After the pastor announced us as husband and wife, we ended our wedding ceremony with praise and worship. The worship was an outward expression of our hearts. The worship team sang and played the tambourines and the drums as we danced a spiritual dance unto the Lord. At the end of the worship, we exited, singing "Celebrate...sing unto the Lord a new song." I marched out of the sanctuary, smiling and crying, my heart filled with gratitude for God's faithfulness and the love Samuel and I shared.

I felt thankful knowing we were walking in obedience to Jesus Christ. However, I knew our marriage would be tested. Satan would come against us: but, we had the Son of the Living God standing for and in us. God spoke to my heart and told me that Samuel and I would have a ministry together, and that we would glorify God through our lives.

Scripture that addresses the reality of struggles in this life coupled with the reality of Christ's love present with us in all circumstances is 1 Corinthians 13:12-13: "For now we see through a glass, darkly; but then face to face: now I know in part; but then shall I know even as also I am known. And now abideth faith, hope, charity, these three;

but the greatest of these is charity.

Samuel married me having full knowledge of my HIV condition. Our marriage was a gift from God, but that did not prevent Satan from trying to destroy it in every way possible. I would love to say that after the marriage consummation everything was perfect, but that wouldn't be honest. I believe that God gave us a glimpse of the expected end that He would bring us to, and then took us back to the beginning--to mold us and change us according to His purpose for our lives.

Samuel accepted his call to the ministry in 1992. His greatest love is outreach ministry and prison ministry. I was also called into the ministry. As ministers of the gospel, we became a threat to the devil. We quickly learned that the nuptial promises we made would be tested.

As a newlywed, I faced obstacles from my past. The scars of my past made it hard for me to be intimate with Samuel through lovemaking. I would often panic and become jittery. Two months after being married, I became pregnant. I took the home pregnancy test and later scheduled a doctor's appointment which confirmed my pregnancy. This visit was deeply emotional due to the doctor's blunt delivery of hard news: "This pregnancy could possibly kill you, kill the baby, or kill you both." My husband and I sat quietly, as the doctor calmly suggested that I consider terminating my pregnancy in light of the risk to my life.

On that day I walked out of the doctor's office heartbroken. The thought of having an abortion delivered a devastating blow to my life. I found it impossible to process my feelings through the inner turmoil I felt. Samuel and I clung to each other. I began to struggle with the idea of having an abortion. Samuel said he believed and trusted

God, but the choice was mine to make. We went to our pastor for prayer about our situation. I respected my pastor, Bishop Bryan because he never spoke hastily, but always pointed us to Jesus. Others also interceded in prayer for us.

However, with my finite mind, I anxiously made the decision to do what seemed logical. Shortly after the visit to the doctor, I made an appointment to get an abortion. Meanwhile, we continued to pray. I spent many sleepless nights thinking of abortion.

During this time of mental anguish, God brought a co-worker, Ellen, into my life. I ended up revealing my situation to her. Ellen, being strong in faith, spoke what God's Word said. She constantly encouraged me and often put healing Scriptures on my desk. Ellen was a Caucasian friend who became as close as my blood sister. God brought Ellen into my life as my partner in faith. Obedient to her call, Ellen quickly opened her spirit and energetically shared her deep faith. Other friends prayed that God would speak to my heart and show me His plan.

Ellen invited Samuel and me to a meeting of a minister, Joe Jordan, who had a special ministry of "joy." During the meeting, people got what Pentecostals call "drunk in the spirit," and many were laughing uproariously. Samuel suddenly burst out in laughter and fell across my lap, overcome with joy. We both knew that something had broken in the spirit realm.

I woke up the next day--my mind crowded with reservations--as I dealt with the hard decision I'd made to abort the life within me. I got up knowing that in just a few hours I would have an abortion. I went downstairs and opened the refrigerator. And as I opened the refrigerator, I thought I felt movement inside my stomach. I touched my stomach, knowing the baby would not move this early in pregnancy. However, this sensation made me aware of the life within me. I ran upstairs, crying and calling out to Samuel, “I can’t do it....I can’t kill our child.” He began to praise God that I did not want to have the abortion. On that day, I chose to agree with him to trust God. We agreed in prayer that we would have our baby and count our child as a gift from God.

A few months later I had an appointment, and they took an amniocentesis test to determine the health and sex of the baby. My spirit was peaceful; I felt relieved with the choice we had made. Two weeks later I received the results from the amniocentesis test. The test revealed I was having a baby girl. We chose to name her Faith because we knew we were having her by faith in God alone. The months passed and I joyfully carried her with anticipation knowing she would be special. One week before the birth of little Faith Nicole, I experienced severe pain in my left leg due to the baby’s pressing on the sciatica nerve.

The anticipated day finally arrived, and on November 5, 1993, our baby girl was born. My doctor performed a cesarean section birth. My daughter, Faith Nicole’s birth, came at 11:00 p.m. -- on my mother’s birthday. My beautiful baby girl weighed six pounds. My heart filled with joy when they placed her on my chest. I cried tears of joy for not aborting my precious little girl. In the delivery room Samuel lifted her up and presented her to the Lord, saying, “Lord, this is our child. We give her back to you to use for your glory...In Jesus Name.”

While in the hospital I thoroughly enjoyed feeding and holding my baby. Samuel and our son Justin came to the hospital every day. We were all excited about the new addition to our family.

However, due to high fevers I experienced, my stay in

the hospital was longer than expected. In fact, one night the doctor came into my room and told me my baby would be released before I would if my fever didn't break. I resisted the idea. That night Samuel stayed by my bedside praying. He was praying when I fell asleep, and when I woke up, he was on the phone praying with Elder Harley from the church. Samuel was a fervent intercessor. On the next day, my child and I were both released from the hospital.

Footprints of Obstacles

∞∞∞

When thou passest through the waters, I will be with thee; and through the rivers, they shall not overflow thee: when thou walkest through the fire, thou shalt not be burned; neither shall the flame kindle upon thee.
Isaiah 43:2

My heart was filled with joy knowing that I did not abort our beautiful baby girl, Faith Nicole. However, I was still experiencing pain in my left leg. My friend Ellen came to visit me two days after I was released from the hospital. She ministered to the necessities of my soul. She ministered and prayed with me for hours. I cooperated with the Holy Spirit searching and opening my heart to Jesus Christ. Together Ellen and I prayed the prayer of faith.

God again comforted me with Scripture at this time: "But he was wounded for our transgressions, he was bruised for our iniquities: the chastisement of our peace was upon him; and with his stripes we are healed" (Isaiah 53:5).

I walked with a limp and the pain in my left leg was so intense and unbearable that it caused me to scream. My medical doctor referred me to a neurologist. They put me on nerve medication, which made it hard for me to function. I experienced muscle spasms and would suddenly drop things. At that point, and continuing for the first six months of our daughter's life, my husband became the primary caregiver.

The first time we took Faith Nicole to church was an overwhelming experience. I walked in with my family; although I was limping my heart was filled with joy. I was grateful because my church family continued to uphold us in prayer. The Assistant Pastor, Elder Covington, preached the sermon that Sunday morning. Afterwards, he came down from the pulpit and took little Faith Nicole and held her up declaring the victory. The church broke out in praise. I began shouting and leaping with my limp. I thanked God for the prayers of the people of God. Through prayer, we overcame the doctor's prognosis which said she could die, I could die, or both of us could die.

I continued to deal with the pain in my leg and soon began to experience other symptoms. In November of 1993, after the birth of our baby, I felt it was time to tell my parents, brothers, and my sisters about having the HIV virus. I wanted them to know that if anything happened to me, Samuel was not the cause. I knew that telling them would be a challenge; I was reluctant because I didn't know how they would react towards Wayne's family. I did not want any animosity between the two families because Wayne infected me with the AIDS virus.

One day I telephoned my oldest brother Jerry and told him about the HIV virus. I heard the devastation in his voice and could hear him crying. I began to cry asking him to get the whole family together and bring them to Washington, D.C. A few weeks after giving birth in November 1993, my family came to Washington, D.C.

On Thanksgiving Day, 1993, my family--along with my husband's family--had Thanksgiving dinner at Israel and Yolanda's home. We enjoyed a wonderful dinner, but my mind was preoccupied with thoughts related to telling my family about my HIV status. We stayed at their home for about three hours, and then my family went home with Samuel and me to our house. When we got home, we talked. I became uptight and nervous and knew it was time--time to tell my mother, father, brothers and sisters about my HIV status.

I nudged Samuel to let him know I was ready. Samuel stood next to me and my mother held the baby. I did not want to look into their faces, because I did not want to see their pain. Looking down, I began, nervously. "I asked Jerry to bring you to Washington, because I want to share something with you." Tears running down my face, I continued. "It is difficult for me to say this, but Wayne infected me with the HIV virus, and I am HIV positive."

The room was quiet, and I looked up and saw how each one in my family reacted. My mother had a look that all mothers have that said, *I knew it all along*. My sister Miriam's eyes bulged, and she looked utterly in shock. My father, a strong man, looked down at the floor and shook his head; he then got up and ran upstairs in tears. I wanted to go and console him, but Jerry persuaded me to leave him alone. I could hear my father sobbing and crying--this hurt me so deeply. I told my family that my life was in God's hands. They felt hurt that I had kept this secret from them for so long. "I did not want to burden you," I told them and then added, "We need you to stand in faith with us." My mother thanked Samuel and told him she was glad that I was not alone. My brother also thanked him and shook his hand.

I let them know that I told Wayne's family soon after the diagnosis because I needed his family to help me take care of him. I asked them not to blame anyone. I often wondered how my family would treat Wayne's relatives since both families lived in the same small town in South Carolina.

To my surprise, some of Wayne's family came over unexpectedly that evening. About ten minutes after telling my family of my condition, two of Wayne's sisters knocked on the door. They were bringing birthday presents for Justin's birthday, which had been a month earlier.

I watched my mother, my father, my sister and brothers show love. They reached out and hugged the sisters of the man who gave me the AIDS virus. I thank God that our families have remained close.

Wayne's family showed unbiased love and were an ongoing source of encouragement. Wayne's sister Verneda called me often, and she told me she had great confidence that I was not going to die. She related a dream she had in which Wayne told her that I would be all right; I would not die. Verneda often gave me Scriptures to encourage me. One night on the phone she shared this verse with me: "If thou wilt diligently hearken to the voice of the LORD thy God, and wilt do that which is right in his sight, and wilt give ear to his commandments, and keep all his statutes, I will put none of these diseases upon thee, which I have brought upon the Egyptians: for I am the LORD that healeth thee (Exodus 15:26).

As I experienced more symptoms and challenges, two of my husband's brothers, Israel and Glenn, would say to me, "Whose report will you believe?" I cried and they would not accept my pity parties but encouraged me to be strong. One day my brother-in-law Glenn and I went to lunch at Union Station. Looking me in my eyes, Glenn said, "Your life is in your hands; whether you live or die depends on you." He told me that I must have faith in God. I became angry because I felt he just did not understand. However, his words stayed in my spirit and grabbed hold of my heart. Samuel's family stood strong in their conviction that "all things are possible with God."

The reality of my being HIV positive greatly affected my mother and father, and my sisters and brothers in South Carolina. At first, I received long-distance calls every night.

"I'm going to have to tell your family that you are not dying." Samuel said this in response to the regular phone calls.

"The news is new," I reminded Samuel. "It changed their lives. It is different than merely hearing about the AIDS virus; they now know someone with the AIDS virus. Their loved one is infected with this disease, and the reality of this news has hit them hard."

My family searched for information to help me in the battle. My brother Jerry brought a juicer and vitamins to build my immune system. Family members became personal advocates and have been instrumental in our victory walk. All along the way, they have helped strengthen us in our declaration of Christ as our Healer.

After telling my family, circumstances did not change. My body continued to go through symptoms and illness. I experienced an awful skin condition that kept me awake the whole night with incessant itching. My health worsened. I walked with a limp for almost one year after the birth of my baby. I constantly confessed the Word of God and played healing Scripture tapes continually. In the face of a seemingly impossible situation, I told myself "by His stripes I am healed." The pain and the limping stopped in October 1994.

In April 1994, when my daughter Faith was six- months-old, I often looked into her deep round eyes that always seemed to sparkle. She was a happy baby and cried only if she needed changing or feeding. She always loved to lie on her father's chest. I knew she would be a daddy's girl.

Within my heart, I trusted and believed that Faith was not infected with the virus. At birth, they did not test her for HIV. They said the test would not be accurate because the baby has the antibodies of the mother.

One day she had a doctor's appointment. The doctor looked at her file and asked me for permission for her to take the AIDS test. I consulted with my husband; we agreed to let her take the test.

A few weeks later we took Faith back to the doctor. I walked into the doctor's office not knowing the results. The nurse took us into an examination room. As we waited, I held onto my faith believing God for a good report. Her pediatrician came in and delivered the news. Our daughter was HIV positive. The news devastated me. I started to wail crying out, "My baby does not deserve this. "Where is this God of love that I serve? She is just a baby!" In that same moment, I began crying, blaming myself. I cried all the way home.

My husband heard the harshness of my words but did not respond. When I got home, I felt I needed to talk to someone. In my despair, I called Mother Watson to tell her about Faith. She listened as I wailed my frustration, and she responded in a caring voice, "I will be praying for you and your family."

I cried throughout the night. The next day, I went to work, troubled and hurt. That morning I went to eat breakfast in the cafeteria with Tanya and Robin, two of my friends and coworkers. They noticed that I was not myself, that I was distracted. Robin asked, "Olivia, what is wrong with you? You're not your cheery self today." She became persistent--knowing that something was wrong. I broke down in tears and told them about my condition and that of my daughter. That day we cried together. They encouraged my heart and began to stand with me in faith. I refocused myself on Christ as my Healer. My husband and I continued being discreet about our situation. I focused on guarding my spirit and continued to resist doubt and fear.

I started to experience even more painful symptoms than before, and I could not sleep at night. In June 1994, I contracted pneumonia. I didn't need to be hospitalized, but I stayed home from work for five days. During that time, I felt as if I had no strength. My body was covered in boils, and I broke out in shingles with painful blisters. I felt as if I wanted to die. In desperation, I scratched the boils into sores. During this time, I mostly stayed in my bedroom upstairs and left the care of my children to my husband.

The week when I was home with pneumonia Yolanda and Betty came over to visit. I lay down in my bed, annoyed by an unbearable itch and boils. I felt creepy when I touched the boils. Yolanda rubbed Benadryl over my body to soothe the itch from the boils. Then Yolanda and Betty prayed for me. However, in my despair, I could not pray. They continued praying and interceding on my behalf. Then suddenly I began to pray and my prayer changed to praise. I found myself praying in the spirit speaking in unknown tongues. When we finished praying, they said they had seen death on me. I thanked God for the power of prayer.

A few days later, I received a phone call from another sister-in-law, Jeannette, who worked at a local hospital as an AIDS counselor. She said she heard I had had pneumonia, and then added, "You are blessed. I know many who died of pneumonia." She knew this from her experience as an AIDS counselor. "You better give God the glory," she reminded me. God used Jeannette to remind me of God's power and blessing on my life. On that day Jeannette and I prayed and glorified God for keeping me.

God used her to remind me of the reality of His power and His greatness.

Despite my suffering, I longed to be a good mother to my children and wife to my husband. I became concerned with the struggles we faced as a family. I watched my son Justin as he looked at his sister and me. I saw the concern in his eyes. I felt my husband's burden as he prayed for the healing of his daughter and his wife. I held my daughter in my arms, looking down on her and knowing I gave her the virus. However, in the midst of all these concerns, I wanted my family to maintain a normal family life.

On November 6, 1994, we celebrated Faith's first birthday and dedicated Faith to God through a dedication ceremony. We made a commitment to raise our children in the fear of God: "Train up a child in the way he should go: and when he is old, he will not depart from it" (Prov. 22:6). We invited our family and Faith's Godparents Lawrence Sr. and Ann H. Davis to witness the occasion. Bishop Bryan the pastor prayed and dedicated Faith to God. He pronounced spiritual affirmations over her life. The service ended in prayer for our family. After the dedication, we celebrated her first birthday party.

My husband and I felt that our family was complete having a son and a daughter. We sought to give our children the basic elements for a healthy and happy childhood. Justin was ten years old and Faith was one. Justin watched his sister and me attentively and often asked if we were okay. He helped any way he could. I became very concerned about Justin's emotional stability as well as my daughter's well-being. Nevertheless, we stood on the Word of God.

Faith was active and happy toddler . I watched this little life blossom into a life of faith. I knew she was a gift from God. The anointing of God was soon obvious in her life. God had ordained her within my womb. Jeremiah 1:5 came to mind: "Before I formed thee in the belly I knew thee; and before thou camest forth out of the womb I sanctified thee, and I ordained thee a prophet unto the nations." She would run through the house with her hands lifted up shouting and singing victory songs. I saw her as a warrior.

I began to deal with the stresses and concerns related to my daughter's HIV status. *What about when she started school?* I would think to myself. *What would her life be like then*? I had heard horror stories about HIV children being kicked out of school and taunted. I began to pray that God would give her a spirit to overcome every obstacle.

Telling the World

∞∞∞

For we walk by faith, not by sight.
2 Corinthians 5:7

During 1994 and 1995, I suffered from one physical attack after another. My husband and I prayed for wisdom and guidance regarding sharing our burden with others. We told those the Lord placed on our hearts to tell. I believed that God was not a God of chance but a God of purpose. I believed he used those he placed in my life to help me walk and see God's miracle footprints. We obeyed God and disclosed my illness as we felt led. We did not know how people would react.

In 1995, when Justin was ten years old, I told him about my condition. I had previously told him only of the secondary cause of his father's death, kidney disease, not AIDS. As his mother I had wanted to shield him from the pain. But now I felt the time had come to disclose things to Justin more fully. I found the right time and sat down with him. I began to tell him about AIDS and how it is transmitted. I explained the truth that his father died of AIDS and infected me, and I gave it to Faith. As I talked to Justin, he did not show any emotions--just said quickly when I paused at the end, "Are you finished?"

I answered, "Yes. Just remember Mama loves you very much and everything is going to be all right." I gave Justin a hug as I wondered and wished I could tell what he was feeling or thinking.

Shortly after my talk with Justin, he started having behavioral problems. I felt this was his way of processing the news that his mother and his sister were HIV positive. One Sunday, a few months after telling Justin about my HIV status, he and I were coming home from church alone. I began to question Justin to see if I could get him to talk. I asked if he had any questions or worries about HIV. "Justin," I emphasized, "Do not be afraid. You can ask me anything."

"Am I HIV positive?" Justin asked, "and if you died, who will take care of me?"

I bit my lip in shock, and responded, "Justin, you are not HIV positive. I got the HIV virus from your father when we got back together." I said, "Justin I believe that God will heal me. However, I wrote in my will that your uncle Jerry would take care of you." I then, at that moment, began praying out loud asking God to bless my son. Looking over at Justin in the front passenger's seat, I grabbed his hand and said, "We are all going to be all right."

After telling Justin, my husband and I began to tell others about my HIV condition. In 1995 Samuel and I visited Ann H. Davis, Faith's godmother during the Christmas holidays. She was recuperating from surgery at the time. When I first became pregnant, the Lord led my husband and me to ask her to be Faith's godmother. We were aware of the spiritual strength she gave our family. On the evening we visited her home, I told her of the HIV status of myself and her goddaughter. She received the news with self-restraint and said she would believe God with us. Since then she has stood with us through many tests and trials.

I then decided to tell my dear friend, Dyonne. During times of distress, I had resisted her kindness. She pushed beyond the barriers that I had erected and became a true friend. Dyonne would call me and sing songs of encouragement. She unceasingly declared that I was blessed and highly favored. The words that she declared eventually became truth within my spirit. One night Dyonne and I went out to dinner, and I told her about my HIV status. She agreed in prayer and walked with me in faith.

My next disclosure was Justin's godparents, James and Shirley Tucker. One night my friend Yolanda went with me to James and Shirley's home. As I began to share my condition with them, Shirley cried. She then admitted that she had known. James, her husband, sat across the room very still with the look of prayer on his face. During the conversation, my plans of telling only those closest to me changed. Right there in their home, the Holy Spirit prompted me to put down pride and to go public about my condition. With a fresh revelation of God's grace and mercy, shame and pride could not keep me from my next step. I decided to reveal my HIV status to the public.

My husband and I decided that our first public disclosure would be to our church family. However, after telling a few, the news of my HIV status had gotten out. Sister Julia Covington and others planned an appreciation service in my honor. Some misunderstood this, thinking it was because I was dying. Yet, I felt it was a display of love and an opportunity for my husband and me to get our church family to stand with us in faith.

This opportunity came on the first Sunday evening of June 1995, at our annual Women's Day service. On that evening, I received tributes and gifts of honor as the Women's Ministry president. After the tribute and gifts, I stepped to the microphone. On that day, I told them their

Women's Ministry president was a woman with the AIDS virus. At that time, I was thin and frail with an awful skin condition.

I had been their president for four years. The pastor's wife appointed me as their president one year after Wayne's death. This was my first public disclosure. I looked into the congregation--at the women I served and the others that were there. Samuel held my hand, and we spoke of our faith walk. "Every step we take," Samuel said, "is a step to our miracle." On that day my church family became my support group and aided me in my miracle walk. They loved us unconditionally.

I realized I had developed a phobia about how others would treat me after knowing my HIV status. However, on that day I received freedom from the condemnation that satan had hung over my head for years. A veil of shame was lifted. The church opened their arms and gave love and support. I told them that the church has a role to play in this, and other HIV persons would come to the church seeking love and acceptance.

After my confession to my church family, a change occurred. I entered into the rest of God. He brought me to a place of peace where I knew beyond any doubt that He was in control. I found solace that assured me my life and my times were secure in His hands.

Psalm 31:15-16 was one of the Scripture passages that ministered to me. "My times are in thy hand: deliver me from the hand of mine enemies, and from them that persecute me. Make thy face to shine upon thy servant: save me for thy mercies' sake." Another passage was Hebrews 4:9-11: "There remaineth therefore a rest to the people of God. For he that is entered into his rest, he also hath ceased from his own works, as God did from his. Let us labour therefore to enter into that rest, lest any man fall after the same example of unbelief."

After our disclosure of my HIV status, Samuel held tightly to the belief that Christ had the last say. He demanded that we walk by faith and not by sight. We had many trials and challenges in our life. I felt blessed and appreciated having a man of faith by my side. Samuel lifted me up when I got weary. We stood knowing that with each other, and with Christ in the middle, we would make it.

I think of our relationship when I read Ecclesiastes 4: 9-12 : *"Two are better than one; because they have a good reward for their labour For if they fall, the one will lift up his fellow: but woe to him that is alone when he falleth; for he hath not another to help him up Again, if two lie together, then they have heat: but how can one be warm alone ? And if one prevail against him, two shall withstand him; and a threefold cord is not quickly broken."*

We continued fighting for my life and the life of our daughter, Faith Nicole. I continued to go to work and trust in God for strength through every symptom.

Standing in the Eye Wall of the Storm

∞∞∞

And the rain descended, and the floods came,
and the winds blew, and beat upon that house; and
it fell not: for it was founded upon a rock.
Matthew 7:25

I continued on and compared the storms in my life to a natural hurricane which grows from the eye to the eye wall. The eye wall is the most violent part of the hurricane with the strongest and the most destructive winds. I found myself standing in the eye wall of the spiritual storms of my life experiencing one hardship after another.

Satan tried many maneuvers to divert me from God's path of healing and restoration. I was constantly at war with the enemy--the devil--who of course, did not want the purpose of God to come to pass in my life. In the middle of much pain and misery, I had to encourage my soul and speak encouragement to my own mind. "Why art thou cast down, O my soul? and why art thou disquieted in me? hope thou in God: for I shall yet praise him for the help of his countenance." (Ps. 42:5)

Diversions from the enemy came one after the other. For example, one Tuesday night at prayer service, I was praising God with my hands lifted up when suddenly my right arm drew up in pain. My husband and I rushed out of the service. The right side of my face began to twist uncontrollably.

The next day, October 3, 1995, I went to see a

neurologist who took a CAT scan. The neurologist called my husband and me into his office to show us the X-ray. The results showed toxoplasmosis on the left side of my brain. He said that I must begin medication immediately. He said a brain infection was causing the headaches, confusion, and weakness and numbness in parts of my body. My hands shook and it was hard for me to write.

I asked the doctor what my prognosis was with this brain infection. He said unless the infection is treated in time, symptoms can progress. He told us there was no cure, and that I would be on medication the rest of my life.

I tried to process this news of a brain condition and perhaps the loss of my mental faculties. I began to feel frustrated and perplexed. My doctor said I should leave my job. Within a few weeks, I started filling out the forms for disability at the Department of Labor. I had just gotten a promotion and job change within the agency. When I met with my new supervisor, Brenda, in a conference room to go over my job description, I had to tell her that I could not fulfill my duties. I told her about my medical condition, and she started to cry. I tried to comfort her and assured her that I trusted God to heal me.

I later told Angie, another coworker, who had begun to sense something was wrong. One day when we were alone in an office, I told her what the doctors had said. Tears flowed down her cheeks. "Why," she asked, "do bad things happen to good people?"

"It rains on the just as well as the unjust," I replied, "and I am so grateful I have Christ to see me through."

Despite all the physical attacks that came my way, I fought against thinking negative thoughts and refrained from speaking negative words. I also refused to agree with the doctors that I was dying.

I told Samuel that I refused to say--or to write on any forms--that I was dying. I thanked God that I didn't have to answer that question. The doctors filled out the portion of the form dealing with life expectancy, and they indicated I had nine months or less to live. I officially left my job and went on disability on November 30, 1995. My soul at times would become troubled. I found comfort in David's words. "My tears have been my meat day and night, while they continually say unto me, Where is thy God? When I remember these things, I pour out my soul in me: for I had gone with the multitude, I went with them to the house of God, with the voice of joy and praise, with a multitude that kept holyday" (Psalm 42:3-4).

I looked at my life, and I looked at the facts. I had to choose whether to continue to trust God or to give in to despair. I could only lean on God's Word. God instructed me to let my words be few. I put God in remembrance of His words. I studied the witnesses in the Bible who withstood enormous suffering. "*Wherefore seeing we also are compassed about with so great a cloud of witnesses, let us lay aside every weight, and the sin which doth so easily beset us, and let us run with patience the race that is set before us" (Heb. 12:1).*

I reflected on how God had blessed me since Wayne's death. I asked the Lord to use the pain to help me to grow. I realized I had grown, and I took nothing for granted. I kept Rom. 8:28 ever before me. *"And we know that all things work together for good to them that love God, to them who are the called according to his purpose" (Rom. 8:28).* With this Scripture in my heart, I knew that all things would work together for my good, even my failures, and my mistakes.

During these times, I compared my life to that of both Job and the woman with the issue of blood.

This was a lonely time in my life. Jesus Christ became my only source of strength. I had to fight discouragement and logic that said the battle is not worth the fight. I had to fight feelings of purposelessness. I had to face humiliation and ridicule from onlookers. I realized that many of the people around me did not expect me to recover. But praise God, Samuel and I stood strong in faith. We never voiced any doubt.

I witnessed others in the church pass away and go home to be with the Lord. One precious woman who was dear to me, Elizabeth Lloyd, died of cancer. During her sickness, I confided in her about my condition. We would pray and believe God together that we both would be healed. She wanted so much to live, just as I did. I attended her funeral. The devil tried to torment me with the thought that I would be next. It took all the spiritual strength I had to rebuke satan and declare that I would not die, but live and declare the works of the Lord.

Another dear young man, Ronald Holley, went home to be with the Lord, leaving behind a beautiful family. Satan whispered to me that I would leave a beautiful young family behind. After this young man's death, our prayer group went to his home to pray. While there, the Lord instructed me to go to his wife Diane and pray for her personally. I understood her grief; but at the time I felt incapable of ministering to her, because my mind was filled with fear about my own life. Despite my apprehension, I obeyed God and ministered to her. This time of ministry worked twofold. When I told her to give her pain to God, God told me to give my fear to Him. The Holy Spirit gave us comfort, and we were both blessed.

During this time of confronting one obstacle after another, I hid myself in God and in His Word. Nothing mattered to me as much as the presence of God. I found peace and hope in the Old Testament, especially in the book of Habakkuk.

"Although the fig tree shall not blossom, neither shall fruit be in the vines; the labour of the olive shall fail, and the fields shall yield no meat; the flock shall be cut off from the fold, and there shall be no herd in the stalls: Yet I will rejoice in the LORD, I will joy in the God of my salvation. The LORD God is my strength, and he will make my feet like hinds' feet, and he will make me to walk upon mine high places."(Hab. 3:17-19)

I saw no physical fruit of healing in my body. Obstacles plagued me from within and without. In the spirit, I saw our marriage as a rose garden, despite all the attacks the enemy brought against it in the natural world.

I experienced emotional thorns of pain and suffering. These were always battling within and without, and Samuel and I both had to fight them. I became concerned about the battles Samuel fought within himself. "You know I have ruined your life," I would shout at him in times of doubt. I knew Samuel was not HIV, but he had to deal with the pain of my suffering. He would simply remind me that he obeyed God by marrying me, and he said he had no regrets.

At times I felt I brought so much pain and so much suffering to my family. Truthfully, at these times I did not feel the flow of the Holy Spirit. I allowed the streams of living water to become clogged by the debris of the cares of my life. During these times, I encountered wretchedness and exhaustion. I became an introvert and withdrew into silence. I felt separated from others and sometimes walked away from people; and they often walked away from me as well.

I asked God to give me the strength to reach down in

my soul and draw waters out of the wells of my salvation. My only place of safety was in praising God. I would praise Him with all my heart. I needed this experience of worship to survive. Worshiping and praising God became my hiding place. In the presence of God household problems seemed small, financial problems seemed smaller and marital problems appeared even smaller when I entered into true worship. I faced various problems, but with God's grace, they never consumed me. I was able to go on. I truly experienced the awesome power of God's presence in the midst of my trials.

God placed people in my life who strengthened me and offered compassion in my times of need. Family and friends offered love and support to both my family and me. Friends and acquaintances remained unbiased during this hard time; and I believe it was the power of the Holy Spirit that enabled them to show such unconditional love.

Without being biased or prejudiced Deloris, a sister-in-law from my first marriage, said the Lord told her to walk by my side, and do for me whatever the Lord told her to do. God showed me that she often interceded for me in my times of weakness. Deloris prepared meals for my family and me.

Another time I received a call from Cherry Onwubere, a church member offering to cook and to clean my house. God had already prepared my heart to accept her offer gratefully. To that point, I had mostly declined help from those outside the family. However, Sister Cherry came faithfully as a servant of God helping our family in our time of need.

About the time my health began to decline, my sister-in-law, Yolanda, lost her job. She walked with me relentlessly, standing in faith as we cried and prayed together. Also,

Betty a close friend and Samuel's sister, has been a great blessing to me. She helped to take care of my family, and she stood steadfast in faith for my healing and the healing of my daughter. When others died of AIDS, Betty would urge me not to compare my life with theirs, but to stand firm in the confidence that Christ, indeed, was my Healer.

Throughout these hard times, the Lord supernaturally provided all the needs of my family. He became my El Shaddai--The God Who Is More Than Enough. I never took God's blessings for granted. I shall never forget these many blessings of the Lord that came through the hands of compassionate people. They did as the Bible teaches. *"But whoso hath this world's good, and seeth his brother have need, and shutteth up his bowels of compassion from him, how dwelleth the love of God in him? My little children, let us not love in word, neither in tongue; but in deed and in truth". (I John 3:17-18). "Finally, be ye all of one mind, having compassion one of another, love as brethren, be pitiful, be courteous" (I Peter 3:8).*

Worship continued to be a source of strength that allowed me to be open before God. I could open my heart and be transparent before Him hiding nothing but revealing all.

However, it eventually became difficult for me to stand up during worship service. My white blood cells became very low. The doctors started sending me to a hematologist, who specialized in the treatment of blood diseases. The doctor put me on Neupogen to stimulate my white-blood cell production. I gave myself Neupogen injections three times a week.

I wanted to go to an infectious disease specialist, but this was outside my health plan, and my insurance company did not allow it. However, I filed an appeal and was later allowed to do this, for which I praise God.

As a result of seeing a new doctor, I had a blood test called the viral load, a test which indicated that the virus was at a high level in my body. The doctor immediately wrote a prescription for a new medication which we prayed God would use as an instrument of healing for my body. I took this medication by faith in the name of Jesus.

Throughout my own physical suffering, I had to care for my daughter who was beginning to show more symptoms of HIV.

My Christian friends and others encouraged me not to focus on the problems.

Season of Restoration

∞∞∞

Restore unto me the joy of thy salvation. Psalm 51:12
And I will restore *to you the* years *that* the locust
*hath eaten.*Joel 2:24

One Sunday in August 1995, I attended church as usual and cried out to God in worship. It had been eight years since that summer day in 1987 when I received the news that I was HIV positive. I have constantly claimed my healing by faith believing that with God all things are possible.

On this day when the service was over, I began to walk down the middle aisle, and I noticed my friend Karen had begun walking towards me. I hugged her, and she said, "Libby, the Lord told me to tell you that He is going to heal your body." I listened as she spoke. "The Lord will heal you," she said, "during a church service, and you will know when it happens because it will hit you from the crown of your head to the soles of your feet. She said this service would be different from the usual service because there will be a time of ministering to each other."

"I receive my healing in whatever way God chooses," I replied to my friend Karen, "because with God all things are possible."

On Friday, October 4, 1996, the time came just as God promised. I went to an all-night prayer service at the Greater Lighthouse Church. We came together praying and fasting, seeking the face of God. The service started at

10:00 p.m. and ended Saturday, October 5th, at 5:00 p.m.

The service was powerful, and I stood in the glory of Almighty God as we worshiped Him continuously. I was in awe witnessing the service as it flowed under the mighty unction of the Holy Spirit. In the past, I could not stand up during worship because of pain and fatigue. However, on that night the anointing was so great I stood and all the pain and fatigue left.

My dear friend Dyonne conducted the service under the anointing of the Holy Spirit. The service unfolded according to the prophecy that I had received concerning my healing. At one point Dyonne, the worship leader, asked me to come and help her conduct the service. The Holy Spirit prompted me to decline. I became aware in my spirit that I needed to stay in a position to receive. The anointing was not on me to minister to others.

On that night, I cried out to Jesus Christ. At one point in the service, the worship leader asked each person to share a scripture verse. I stood up and read from Psalm 27. "*The LORD is my light and my salvation; whom shall I fear? the LORD is the strength of my life; of whom shall I be afraid?" (vv. 1-2).... One thing have I desired of the LORD, that will I seek after; that I may dwell in the house of the LORD all the days of my life, to behold the beauty of the LORD, and to inquire in his temple. For in the time of trouble he shall hide me in his pavilion: in the secret of his tabernacle shall he hide me; he shall set me up upon a rock."(v. 4-5)*

The Power of Jesus touched me, and he ministered healing to my body. While I was reading Psalm 27:4--"*One thing have I desired of the LORD, that will I seek after; that I may dwell in the house of the LORD all the days of my life, to behold the beauty of the LORD, and to inquire in his temple*"-- I felt it from the crown of my head down to the soles of my feet--just like the prophecy said.

I immediately knew there was a dramatic change taking place in me, but I knew I must not say anything. The prophecy indicated that in the service, we would minister to each other. We did this at the close of the service.

I left the two-day service in awe knowing the Master's healing hand had touched my body. I did not discuss it with anyone, but went home to my family, with the power of God all over me. As I entered my apartment building, I heard beautiful, melodious voices all singing in unison. I heard the singing all the way up to my third floor apartment. When I walked in, I asked Samuel if he had heard the singing, and he said no. I went back to the hallway to see if it was coming from somewhere in the building. I listened at the doors of the other apartments, but didn't hear the remarkable sound coming from any of them. I realized that angels had escorted me home.

I went back into our apartment, thanked Samuel for keeping the children, and told him I'd tell him about the shut-in prayer service after I got some rest. While lying on my bed, a voice spoke to my spirit and said "new skin." My skin was dry and blemished. Sores were all over my body and my feet. I looked at my skin, and although it did not look any different, I said, "Thank you, Lord, I receive new skin." I then went to sleep for about three hours.

I awoke when I heard my sister-in-law Jeannette and her husband Glenn, coming in the door. They said they felt an urgency to come and tell Samuel what the Lord had told them. Their words for Samuel were almost the exact words I had received earlier during the all-night prayer service. I was standing across the room and my sister-in-law looked at me and said, "Libby, God is changing your skin!" She pointed at new skin on my face and arms. I told her that

God had just spoken "new skin" to my spirit as I lay down to rest. We rejoiced together.

I began to see a noticeable change for the better after that night of praying and fasting. My health changed two weeks after the all-night prayer service. One night I was in the bathtub and could scale old skin and sores off the bottom of my feet. My husband and son witnessed my peeling off the boils that were on my hands, feet and back. The boils have never returned. I started gaining weight and an unbearable itch that used to keep me up all night disappeared entirely.

On October 31, 1996, I took a CAT scan. The doctors compared it with two previous CAT scans. The CAT scans showed the toxoplasmosis of my brain was completely gone. My joy knew no bounds, and I was thankful. I shared my victory report with everyone who would listen.

I went back to the doctor for blood work in January 1997. When I called for the test results on Wednesday of the following week, it showed the virus had decreased to such a level that it was undetectable. She said she was pleased with the results. I called Samuel on the cellular phone to give him the good report and to urge him to come home so we could shout the victory together.

I received my first report of an undetectable viral load in January 1997. My T cells had risen from a deadly thirty-five to three hundred and fifty. I declared His greatness to everyone everywhere. Despite the symptoms that tried to attack our bodies over these years, God kept my daughter and me by His mighty power.

In February 1997, I appeared on a panel at Georgetown Hospital in Washington, D.C., with four others. I was given the opportunity to share my experience with about two hundred interns. I asked God to give me the words to say. I was asked to speak first, which I did.

For fifteen minutes I talked about my appreciation for the doctors and those in the medical field. I spoke about my life and the stigma I experienced as a result of having the AIDS virus. I closed my presentation, talking about the value of the doctors, and those in the medical field. I also spoke about my belief in the power of prayer and faith. I told of the blessing of their knowledge and expertise, and I spoke of the blessing of prayer and faith. I asked them to understand the importance of prayer and faith to those who believe in Jesus Christ, and I shared a passage of Scripture: *"If my people, which are called by my name, shall humble themselves, and pray, and seek my face, and turn from their wicked ways; then will I hear from heaven, and will forgive their sin, and heal their land."* (2 Chron. 7:14)

Following all the presentations, I spoke to a believer on the panel. She had lost her husband and sister to AIDS. It was a privilege to represent God.

A few months later I appeared on Channel 7 news. They interviewed me about my health and my faith in God. I discussed my faith and the restoration of my health. With my Bible open and the camera zooming in as my fingers pointed to Isaiah 53:6, I read, "But he was wounded for our transgressions, he was bruised for our iniquities: the chastisement of our peace was upon him; and with his stripes we are healed".

Later in the program they included a study on how your brain works with your faith and the brain's response to prayer and faith. The interview was not long, but I thanked God for the opportunity to represent Him in this way and to give Him the glory. I was later interviewed by someone from a local magazine who wrote an article about my life.

My husband and I have both been blessed to look beyond

our circumstances and minister to others. My husband spent months ministering to a young man who had AIDS. Often, my husband would take him to the doctor for his appointments. He had the opportunity to lead him to Christ a few months before his death.

I was also able to minister to a young lady who had AIDS. My Sunday school teacher Mother Watson, a nurse, gave me the young woman's number so I could call and encourage her. My husband and I would take her to church and sometimes bring her home for dinner. I also visited her in the hospital. I continued ministering to this young woman.

A few weeks before her death I went to a church which happened to be two blocks away from her home. My spirit became troubled, and I could not focus on the service. I asked Nathan, a friend who was also at the service, to walk with me to the young lady's home which was in a bad drug neighborhood. Nathan and I left the service. I did not know what I would see or do when I got there, but I obeyed God. The young woman opened the door, her body frail, and she could barely talk. Nathan and I ministered to her.

A few weeks later she died. I went to her funeral. I met her family. I was told that she was at peace when she died, and that she selected the songs for her funeral.

My faith became stronger through ministering to others. God was being glorified in our lives.

Footprints in My Shadow

∞∞∞

But Jesus called them to him, and said, Suffer little children to come to me, and forbid them not: for of such is the kingdom of God.
Luke 18:16

As time passed, I became more focused on the little footprints of my daughter Faith. Her life placed indelible footprints in my heart through invaluable lessons lived and learned. Faith's life was like a rainbow noticeable from afar. She showed boldness and courage at a young age.

Up to age four, Faith showed little evidence of HIV infection. However, as time passed, symptoms increased. She began to look sick, had poor weight gain, suffered from fungal mouth infections (thrush), and had enlarged lymph nodes and an enlarged liver.

Two weeks before Christmas, December 1997, I took Faith to the doctor. She had a cold and cough that seemed to be getting worse instead of better. The radiologist took an X-ray that revealed pneumonia in her left lung, causing the oxygen level to be low. The doctor sent her to the hospital immediately.

I stayed with my daughter day and night. A week passed, and her oxygen level remained unstable. At one point the doctor took her off the oxygen machine, but her oxygen was still low. On the sixth day, on a Saturday, the doctors gave her a transfusion to boost her immune system. That night, Faith's blood pressure dropped. Her body began to jerk, and she screamed in agony and pain. I frantically called the nurse who held her down. Medication was given through her IV. I looked at my baby and became terrified.

I then called my husband to tell him what was happening. "I am on my way," was his first response. However, he suddenly changed his mind and said, "Let's pray over the phone and watch God move." We prayed and at the end of the prayer Samuel said, "My daughter will be released from the hospital tomorrow." The nurse came in frequently during the night monitoring her. I watched as Faith became less frantic and her blood pressure stabilized.

The next day Samuel came to the hospital, and the doctor told us that Faith may have to spend Christmas in the hospital. I sat in a chair by Faith's bed. I prayed and laid my head on the side of her bed and went to sleep. When I woke up, I noticed the oxygen tube was out of Faith's nose. I immediately woke my husband and pointed at the monitor which showed her oxygen level at 90 percent. Faith's oxygen level remained stable, and they decided to release her around 7:00 p.m. I was thrilled knowing my daughter would be home before Christmas!

One week later, Christmas 1997, we had a family dinner at our home. After dinner, we began singing songs. A bit later I asked Faith, "What did God do for you?"

"God brought me home from the hospital to be with my family," she quickly responded. Prompted by Faith's comment, her Godmother Ann H. Davis and Faith started singing, "I got something to thank the Lord for." Faith told everyone that God had brought her home from the hospital. She began to live up to her name.

My son was now thirteen and my daughter was four. Although we had issues, we were a typical family with a typical family life. Justin's focus was on video games. Faith showed her charisma as being the baby in the family. She began singing songs and often ran through the house shouting and praising God. One day when she was four-years-old, she paused and said, "Mama, let's pray." Immediately the thought *a little child shall lead them* came to mind.

Faith's condition continued to improve. She responded well to the medicine. At first giving her medicines was a struggle. She hated the taste and always cried and resisted. One time she resisted so much that my husband had to hold her down. She cried and bit her tongue causing it to bleed. That was it for Samuel; he refused to do it again. It became so stressful when I gave medicine to Faith that I went to the pharmacist for advice. The pharmacist suggested cocoa and cola syrup to mask the bad taste, and it worked.

In August 1998 Faith started kindergarten. We lived in a three-bedroom apartment. Faith constantly declared at age five, "By his stripes, I am healed." At the time her favorite song was "Shake the devil Off." While singing this song, she would take her little hands and shake the devil off. She would take her feet and stomp, putting the devil under her feet. I watched Faith stand as a little warrior for Jesus Christ.

In February 1998 we moved into our home in Fort Washington, Maryland. I stayed at home and my husband worked for Maret School in Washington, D.C. My son Justin was in the eighth grade. Faith Nicole had started first grade during the school year 1998-1999. I walked her to and from school. She loved school and played well with her peers. She often invited the neighborhood kids over to play sharing what she had, including her father. Faith felt her father could fix anything. One day Faith had a group of her friends standing in line so her father could fix their broken bicycles. When I saw it I laughed calling her a young witness for Jesus Christ helping others.

Faith continued to do well throughout that school year (1998-1999) until the last day of school. On that day, I watched as she walked down the sidewalk. I noticed that her knee was swollen, and she seemed to be in pain. I took her to the doctor, and they admitted her into the hospital for surgery. They wanted to drain any infection or fluid from around the knee.

Before Faith went to surgery Margie Smith a sister and a friend from church came to Holy Cross hospital to pray for Faith. Before performing surgery, they gave Faith a sedative. My husband and I and the hospital chaplain were in the room. My husband held her hand, and she looked up at us and began to sing, "I'm not afraid; Jesus is with me and His angels are all around." She then looked at us and said, "I love you. Give me a kiss." We gave her a kiss. Then she said, "Let us pray." After my husband prayed Faith continued singing.

A woman in the next room who overheard her came in and said, "I just wanted to see this little angel."

"God is going to use that little girl," the chaplain added. Faith stayed in the hospital for a few days.

When we got home Faith would answer the phone. One day I listened as she was talking to my pastor's wife. "Mother Bryan," she said, "God healed me and brought me home from the hospital." I continued to listen as she added, "If I die and go to heaven I'm still healed." Faith's words stirred and startled me. I found myself thinking *she is just a child.* On that day I was assured and convinced of her deep awareness of God at six years old.

In 2000, I dealt with the untimely death of my father

Jerry Green, Sr, as well as Faith's medical care challenges, and health plan contract changes. The Food and Drug Administration removed the medicine Faith was taking from the market. With the changes, we needed to adjust to new medicines, doctors and nurses, as well as to a new hospital and clinic. This change made me angry because the medicine seemed to be working for our daughter. I felt she was a child being treated as an object because of medical insurance and contracts.

The day I took Faith to her first scheduled appointment with the new doctors, I walked into the office angry. I did not want to accept the changes. I prayed, and God reminded me that Faith was in His Hands. I worked with her team and soon developed a relationship with them. Together, we were all concerned about what was best for my daughter.

By the beginning of the school year 1999-2000, Faith began experiencing other symptoms. She tired easily walking to and from school. Her attention span was short, and her reading level was low. With my consent, she was placed in the special needs program in school. During the course of the year, she overcame the obstacles. In fact, in the school year 2001, Faith received an achievement certificate award for the most improved, and later was placed in her regular classes.

Faith endured her medical challenges while still living fervently for Christ. She started being hospitalized more frequently. She developed infections, and she needed frequent blood transfusions. To fight infection in her body, Faith needed a home IV port placed in her arms, and I had to give her medicines intravenously three times a day. I lived day by day adjusting my life as needed.

My husband and I stood on the Word of God; Faith stood on the Word of God. She kept a fighting spirit and lived by faith every day. She believed God for her healing and her trust was in Him alone. One Saturday night at 3:00 a.m., Faith developed a fever of 104 degrees. I immediately called urgent care. The doctor told me to give her Motrin and place her in some cool water. My husband and I placed her in the tub, and she cried, "Mommy and Daddy, I want Jesus, I want Jesus." She continued to call on the name of Jesus. My husband and I prayed and around five o'clock the fever was gone.

The next morning I got up and told Faith that we were not going to church that day.

"I am not going to let the devil win Mommy; I want to go to church," she announced.

Even though I was tired, I could not resist her bravery and persistence, and we all went to church. Faith knew her strength was in serving God and others. She developed her gift of singing and became a part of the dance ministry team. At the time she was the youngest member.

Faith was sensitive to prayer. She responded to the altar call if she felt she needed prayer. She asked my husband and me to pray if she felt pain in her body. She often prayed for others. One night I began to pray for my husband when Faith was asleep in bed with us. Faith woke up when she heard me praying and laid her little hands on her father and prayed with me. After the prayer, she went back to sleep.

Faith was strong in standing her ground in what she was taught and did not mind being different. My husband and I refused to buy her Harry Potter's books because of the sorcery, magic spells, and warlocks, written about in the books. A Harry Potter book was given as a reading assignment in school. She came home from school and said, "I told my teacher that I could not read Harry Potter's books." The next day I wrote a note, and the teacher gave her another reading assignment. She also stood her ground and refused to celebrate Halloween with the class.

One day Faith called me into her room. "Mommy," she said through tears, "God spoke to me. Jesus said He is going to heal me. He said I will not have to take anymore medicine." I looked into her eyes and saw the sincerity of her tears. I knew she had had an experience with God. "Write down what God said to you in your diary," I encouraged her.

One day Angela Ferguson called me at home and gave me a prophecy she received from God about my daughter's life. She told me the prophecy and prayed with me. My spirit was in awe because it only confirmed what had been was spoken in my spirit. She wrote the prophecy down and later gave me a copy of it. I watched as it happened in my daughter's life. The prophecy follows--a "Prophecy Given by Evangelist Ferguson Concerning My Daughter Faith--spoken on May 24, 1999, at 10:00 a.m."

"I call her Faith. Even as I thought on Samuel, Isaac, John the Baptist; even my Son so did I think on her before she was. Even I was glorified through them, so shall I be glorified through her. For I have called her forth unto myself for my purpose and for my glory. Be not dismayed, be of good cheer for I shall bring forth a pure harvest in her in due season. Know that I am God. I make no mistakes. See my glory for I am God."

After this spoken word of prophecy, Faith endured more medical challenges. Nevertheless, she had made up her mind to sing and dance for Jesus Christ. When she was weak she said, "I can do all things through Christ that strengthens me." With determination, she continued to dance in the dance ministry in the church. She was a soloist. Her songs demonstrated her life. Faith would sing in church programs, in a nursing home, in the hospital, for the pastor, and for her father before he preached. She became devoted to her ministry of singing.

One day she heard "Alabaster Box" by CeCe Winans on the radio. Faith was inspired and wanted to sing that song. On the following day, Faith and I went to the Christian bookstore. She sat at the table with headphones on listening to songs and decided she wanted to buy "Alabaster Box" and "I Know My Redeemer Lives." I told her I was only going to buy one tape and one soundtrack. A lady in the store happened to notice how serious Faith was and told us God had told her to buy the other song and soundtrack for Faith. She said she wanted to plant a seed in this child's ministry.

Faith diligently learned the songs she was inspired to learn, and they became the songs most often requested for her to sing. One night the pastor called and said he wanted her to sing before he preached. Faith was thrilled and said, "I have to sing and do my best for my Bishop." She then went into her room and practiced. The next day she sang "I Know My Redeemer Lives."

"Is that Faith singing?" my sister-in-law Betty asked as we were coming down the hall at church. I hurried into the sanctuary to see her singing. Whenever she had the opportunity, she would stand boldly before the congregation singing songs such as "Holy Spirit Come in This Place," "What God Has for Me, It is for Me," "Take the Shackles off My Feet, So I Can Dance," "Alabaster Box," and "I Know My Redeemer Lives." I began to notice that every song Faith chose to sing seemed to represent her life and her relationship with Christ. She would always choose the song she sang. It started when she was a toddler, with her first song, "Shake the devil Off."

My family was active in church life, and as a family we lived, laughed, and loved together. I recall a time of laughter when my husband, son, daughter, and I sat down in our living room. We were having a family night--an open discussion to talk about what you want to change or don't like. Justin responded, "I want us to spend more time together as a family."

Faith chimed in seriously, "I don't like when the toilet seat lid is up, whenever I go into the bathroom" At that very moment we all laughed. It was those moments of laughter that kept us going.

We frequently went out of town to visit my family in Florence, South Carolina. We all adjusted and dealt with the effect AIDS brought upon our lives.

Justin was sixteen and Faith was now seven. I carried a special burden for my son and dealt with the stress of wondering how he felt. I often stayed at the hospital with my daughter--day and night when I needed to. As a result, I was unable to spend quality time with Justin.

Faith's health continued to decline. She was often home schooled through Prince George's public school system. She was experiencing more difficulties and began to ask questions about her medical condition. I asked God to give us the courage to tell her. I found a helpful book, which dealt with a mother telling her child about the HIV virus.

One night I sat down with Faith and told her about this terrible disease that was in her body. She asked, "Mommy how did I get AIDS?" I looked at her in deep remorse and told her that I gave it to her. I held her close crying saying I am sorry that I gave you AIDS. Her response showed her faith in God. She said "Mommy you did not do this: the devil did this. She then said what she said before "if I die and go to heaven I am still healed." I was astounded at her courage that encouraged me.

However, at times, I dealt with the pain of regret. In every way, I wanted to take away all her pain and suffering and put it on myself. She had done nothing to deserve this, and I knew I could handle it if she would not have to suffer. It was easier to deal with my suffering. But when it came to Faith's suffering, I felt a spirit of dissatisfaction towards myself. I had to deal with my inner thoughts--*if only I had done this or done that.* I did not feel the freedom to discuss my regrets to anyone. I felt as if I was allowing regret to imprison my life through my thoughts and emotions. I had to walk in the anointing of God that gave me the ability to live beyond regret.

Faith later had to deal with her peers. One day I heard her talking on the phone to one of her friends from school. Her friend asked why she was out of school so much. Faith answered, "because I have AIDS." I quickly went into her room and told her to hang up the phone. I told her not to tell people. I later called the girl's mother and asked her to ask her daughter not to tell anyone because I did not want my daughter picked on.

One day Faith was approached by two children from church. "Faith, I know you got AIDS," one little boy said. She came crying to her father and me. I told her they did not mean any harm, and I later talked to their parents. Faith faced every challenge as a warrior. One day she said of herself, "I am an evangelist." I watched, and she did indeed prove herself to be an evangelist. Our pastor Bishop Bryan also called her a little evangelist.

From November 2002 until August 23, 2003, Faith's health worsened. She developed anemia and needed several blood transfusions. With her T cells very low, she was home schooled more often. Drug resistance became an issue. She was given a viral counts test to help determine the aggressiveness of the disease. The test showed the disease to be at dangerously high levels in her system. The doctor said she was born with a more virulent version of HIV. The drugs were not working, and there were not many options left. Faith's medical team tried all pediatric medicines for HIV. They even suggested giving her medications that were not yet FDA approved for children.

I took Faith to the doctor and Mary Lou, the Nurse Practitioner, talked to me about my daughter's critical condition. I was distraught and asked if she was telling me to give up. She answered no, but I began to feel defeat within my spirit. Before leaving the doctor's office that day, I talked to Jill, Faith's social worker. She encouraged me to stay positive and remain strong. As she talked, God brought scriptures to my mind to encourage me. I was thankful that God used someone to help me and look to Him.

One day my husband and I, along with Faith's godmother, met with our daughter's health-care team. Faith's health continued to decline, and the doctors said decisions needed to be made. In the face of our bleak circumstances, my husband and I agreed that we would do everything we could to extend Faith's life. In October 2002, a feeding tube was placed in her stomach. In November 2002, Faith was admitted to the hospital with a high fever and was tested for meningitis. I waited, praying, and the test came back negative.

While Faith was in the hospital, her name was submitted to the Make-A-Wish Foundation. When her social worker told me, I felt nervous pangs in my stomach. I knew these were the last wishes of dying children. I pushed my feelings aside and allowed Faith to make her wish. Faith's wish was to go to Florida. We planned our trip for

April 2003.

Faith stayed in the hospital for two weeks and was released. After coming home, she was eager to get back to school. Her care team asked me if I wanted someone to talk to her classmates and educate them on the feeding tube. I agreed and they did. Her classmates treated her well and were cautious about not hurting her. I took Faith to school every day.

I often slept in her bedroom in the other bed monitoring the feeding machine. Faith seemed to adjust well to the feeding tube, and wrote in her diary, "Thank God no more nasty medicine." She was happy I could put the medicine in the tube.

One day I had a worship video playing in the living room, while I cooked and her father was in the basement. I heard her crying. When I asked what was wrong, she said, "Mommy, I feel Jesus all over me, and I want the Holy Ghost. We told her she had the Holy Ghost.

I watched my daughter and saw the power of God being manifested in her! She was small and frail, yet a big God lived inside her!

Please excuse me while I take a praise break! Thank you Lord for Your goodness and mercy. I thank You for how Faith showed forth Your power through the life she lived. I thank You that Faith called on Your Name in her times of need. I thank You for how You used Faith to strengthen the faith of others. To God, I give all the glory. In Jesus' name Amen.

Yet, Holding On

∞∞∞

For I the LORD thy God will hold thy right hand,
saying unto thee, Fear not; I will help thee.
Isaiah 41:13

Two months before our trip to Florida, the Greater Lighthouse church hosted a concert featuring Linda Sutton and Sharon Curtis. They ended their concert by singing one final song along with Faith. Faith stood between two great experienced soloists. Sharon had already recorded a CD. Linda was working on a CD production. Together they sang “Alabaster Box” with Faith, Faith’s favorite song. I watched and listened in awe as she sang bravely under the anointing. I was overjoyed watching my little girl sing. Others stood as I sat stunned because--I had heard her sing many times--but this was different. She reared back in confidence holding the microphone and repeatedly singing “you don’t know the cost of the oil in my alabaster box.” I began to weep because I knew she was conveying this from her spirit. My husband said he was amazed and that she held her own with the best. After the service, many commented saying they have never heard her sing like that.

It was getting close to the date of our scheduled trip to Florida. Before the trip, I took Faith to the doctor. They were concerned about her health and her ability to travel. After consultation and a medical examination, the doctors allowed her to travel. On the trip Faith would require overnight nursing care.

A week before the trip two representatives from the Make-A-Wish Foundation came to our home. We had a going-away party for Faith. I invited Faith's friends. My sister-in-law, Jeannette, brought her daughter, Jasmine to the party. Jeannette looked at Faith and said she could tell that Faith was in the end stage known as wasting. I immediately dismissed the thought and my mind filled with resentment. *How dare she come into my house and all but tell me my daughter is dying?* I refused to believe my daughter was dying, and I fought fearlessly for the healing and restoration of her body.

The time came for us to go to Florida. On April 13, 2003, a limousine picked up my family and took us to the airport to fly to Kissimmee, Florida. We stayed in a cottage for one week and enjoyed all the amenities at the resort. We went to Kissimmee, Florida and Faith mastered the rides in bravery. She chose to ride on the scariest rides at Disney World. I did not want to ride them.

"Mommy, you got to face your fears," Faith said. I finally agreed and rode. Faith and her father enjoyed the rides. However, Justin and I did not.

When we returned from our trip Faith continued to need home-nursing care. She completed the school year and passed. She was happy she would be going to the sixth grade. Faith was very smart and all testing showed that even though she was partly home schooled, she kept up academically and was up to grade level with her classmates.

On May 21, 2003, the home-care nurse and I took Faith to the doctor. After doing the blood work the doctors wanted to admit her to the hospital because her potassium was low. Faith immediately got upset and protested.

"Mommy, please do not let them put me in the hospital."

"Baby," I said, "it will only be for a few days." From that point, the storms intensified in my life and in the life of my family. I held on during the rough storms that only grew stronger. I found myself weary to the point of exhaustion, yet standing. Obstacles and trials washed over me like waves in a surging sea.

After Faith was admitted to the hospital, I stayed by her bedside day and night. We would often pray together. The visitation team from our church would come and serve her Holy Communion. If anyone came and prayed with her, Faith would lift up her hands. The nurses and doctors gave her special care. The doctors would sit on her bed holding her hands to let her know that they cared. Many times I watched the display of compassion and love from the nurses. I saw their love as the hands of God being extended.

A few weeks after Faith was admitted to the hospital, my son Justin graduated from high school. On the day of his graduation Faith had a fever, so I called my friend Margo to sit with Faith. When we returned, Faith had made her brother a card. The card read, "Yea, Justin you did it!" She was still thinking of others.

Faith's health continued to decline. Her abdomen swelled to twice its size. Then she was diagnosed as having chronic pancreatitis, something rare in children. My friend Julia brought me information from the Internet on pancreatitis. Julia and Faith's Godmother Ann became my ears and helped me to comprehend when I dealt with the doctors. Faith was still on oxygen, and they began to give her pain medication.

The doctors were concerned about the size of her abdomen and the stress this could place on her internal organs. They decided to place a tube in her stomach to drain the fluid. It broke my heart to see her change before my very eyes. She had been in the hospital for almost two months.

One night around 3:00 a.m., Faith sat up in bed, waking me, and said, "Mommy, please call my daddy."

"Faith, he is at home asleep," I answered quietly.

"Mommy," she insisted, "please call my daddy."

She really needed to talk to her daddy. I then called her father saying your daughter needs to talk to you. I gave Faith the phone.

"Daddy," she said, "I hear you." "Daddy, I hear you praying."

"Yes," her daddy answered, "I am on my knees praying for you."

I cried because through the spirit, she could hear her father praying and at that exact moment, she wanted to call him. God was proving His power to me.

However, in the middle of our spiritual experiences, I began to notice that Faith's demeanor changed. Sometimes she became irritable with the nurses and would later apologize.

She continued to want to connect with others. One day Jackie and her children came to the hospital to visit with Faith. Although she was weak, playing with them seemed to give her peace. When they left, Faith said, "I am glad that I have friends."

From that point on Faith's health worsened. One day her doctors took my husband and me into a conference room. We listened as they gave us the grave prognosis concerning Faith's health.

"Your daughter is a sick little girl," the doctor said. However, he and the medical team vowed that they would do all they could to extend Faith's life. Her only hope was for them to inject her with medicine that had not been

FDA approved. I had reservations as the side effects were life threatening. The doctors wanted to ease my concerns and suggested that I talk to a mother whose child was taking the same medicine. The mother came and talked to me at the hospital and said her daughter was taking the injections and was doing well with minimal side effects. We then agreed to allow our daughter to take the injections.

One night as my husband, my son and I sat in her room. Faith suddenly cried out, “Do you see it? Do you see the rivers? Do you see the flowers?” I felt she saw heaven and immediately picked up my Bible and began reading scriptures to her. My husband sat in the corner praying, and he afterward read scriptures to her as well. We read God’s Word to her throughout the night. I prayed, inwardly crying, “God, please don’t take my daughter.”

The weeks passed and Faith's illness progressed and became more critical. One morning I awoke and looked into her eyes and saw a glazed look. I called the nurse, and she said everything was all right. However, I knew something was wrong. On that morning, I kept telling them something was not right. I waited for my husband to arrive, and I began to cry. My friend Julia happened to walk in. She laid her hands on my shoulder and took an authoritative stand and told them to call Faith’s doctor. The doctor came in and said he would send her to the Pediatric Intensive Care Unit. My husband arrived an hour later, and Faith stayed in that lethargic state for hours. We stood by her bed praying. Her vitals became stable, and they decided against putting her in the Pediatric Intensive Care Unit.

Two weeks later I sat with Faith as she lay in her hospital bed. In the middle of the day, around noon, she said: “Mommy call my daddy.” I knew from experience how to respond. I called her father and gave her the phone.

"Daddy," she said, "I need you to come to the hospital now." He told her he was coming.

I sat by Faith's bed waiting for Samuel. She was not showing any signs of distress. Suddenly, she went into code blue pulmonary arrest and the alarm went off. Her blood pressure dropped, as did her oxygen level. I stood by and watched as they called a code blue and the medical staff quickly rushed in and filled her room. The staff worked to revive Faith. They needed to incubate her immediately. Everything was happening so quickly before I knew it she was being transported to the Pediatric Intensive Care Unit. All of this happened before my husband arrived. I kept crying, "Jesus, Jesus." I did not want my child to die. My husband arrived, and the waiting room soon filled with family and friends.

They took X-rays, which showed infection had developed in her lungs. When Faith was placed in ICU, I could not stay by her side. Visitation time was limited. I stayed in the waiting room until I was allowed to see her again, all the while longing to be by her side.

After one week, they took Faith off the ventilator, and she was breathing on her own. My mother and brother drove from South Carolina on a Saturday, and Faith talked to them. I was thankful my little girl seemed to be doing better. I was told she would soon go back to a regular room.

After my mother and brother left, my daughter continued to talk, and all seemed well. A patient next to her had a horrible cough, and I asked the nurse if they could move Faith since her immune system was already compromised, but they couldn't. No more private rooms were available.

On Sunday, the following day, they took X-rays. The

doctor said she needed to go back on the ventilator. My emotions were becoming a roller-coaster ride. I could not understand how she could change so fast.

Faith did not want to go on the ventilator; she pleaded and cried. My husband cried and asked Faith to please do it for us. She finally agreed. We asked her to be strong. Before the procedure, my husband and I stood by her bedside. My husband began singing "What a Mighty God we Serve."

"No, Daddy," Faith quickly said, "sing the blood song." He then sang to her, "There is power in the blood." Faith looked up.

"Daddy," she said, "if I die, the devil still won't win."

"You will not die," I said, quickly turning my head, so she could not see the tears. They asked us to leave, but as I left her words plagued my mind "if I die…the devil still won't win."

Every day they would take X-rays of her lungs. Her lung tissue was hardened they said. They moved Faith into a private room in ICU where I played healing scriptures and worship music continuously. I placed pictures of her on the wall so everyone who came into her room could see her as she was.

I was expecting my daughter to live. Almost one week later Faith's body swelled to twice her size. The doctor took us into a conference room and said there was no hope of recovery, and that Faith would never come off the ventilator. They wanted to take her off the ventilator, so she could spend her last hours with her family.

I left the conference room and walked back into the waiting room feeling empty like my insides had been pulled out. I went into the room and curled up in a chair. The news seemed too much to bear. Faith's psychologist and social worker came to see me. I was heartbroken. Dr.

New, her psychologist, took me outside to get some air. We sat under some trees, and I could feel a breeze from the trees.

"How do you feel?" she asked.

"Angry," I said. "I don't understand. Faith was admitted for low potassium, and now she is dying....I can't put another child in the ground," I cried out. "I just can't."

She responded, "Samuel asked me to talk to you because he is worried about you." Talking could not ease the pain I was feeling.

Samuel began calling the family and told them the doctors were giving up on Faith. By the afternoon all our family was in the waiting room. They were permitted to go in and see Faith. They came out crying and terrified. She did not look at all like herself. After everyone saw her, we gathered for prayer.

However, I changed my mind and told the doctors not to take her off the ventilator. I emphasized that I wanted them to do all they could to save her life. The doctor stressed it would be a matter of time and she would never breathe on her own. Nevertheless, I chose to keep believing. While she was in ICU, many church friends came to pray with us and often ministered to others. I was always blessed to have family and friends by my side. One night two of my friends Bernadette and Carrie stayed with me the entire night.

I watched with horror as our daughter deteriorated, for I still had hope that she would recover. I held tight to hope despite all her challenges. It broke my heart to see her with so many tubes and IV lines. She had a breathing tube in her mouth connected to a ventilator and was in a medication induced coma. It was a sight too horrible to bear. I kept healing scriptures playing in the room. The nurse always said there was such peace in her room. By this time, Faith had been in the hospital since May 21, 2003, and she had gone into ICU at the end of July 2003.

One Sunday morning around the first week of August 2003, a miracle happened. Mary Lou, who had been Faith's nurse, came to visit her while Samuel and I were at church. When we arrived later that afternoon, Mary Lou eagerly told us what had happened.

She said she walked into the room and the television was on. The minister on the television was preaching on faith. She said the preacher said faith three times in his message, and that when he said faith the third time, Faith opened her eyes. She said she knew it was a miracle. I began to wonder who turned the television on. A few days later, Faith started to talk with the tube in her throat.

Faith wanted desperately to get out of ICU. Often when we needed to leave her room, she would have her arms outstretched, crying out to us with the tube in her throat.

"Mommy and Daddy, please don't leave me." I looked into her deep brown eyes and felt helpless. My husband said it broke his heart.

"I promised I would not leave her," he murmured. "I let her down."

Faith appeared to get better. The doctors told us that they were going to put a tracheotomy tube in her throat. Then they would transfer her to the Children's Home in Washington D.C. I went to the hospital library to get information on the tracheotomy tube. This procedure gave me hope, and I was so happy it appeared my baby was beating the odds. Several pastor friends came to pray for Faith.

However, Faith seemed distant and uninterested as if her mind was in another place. I would talk to her about coming home. She gave no response. It got to the point she would pretend that she was asleep. When I walked out of the room and looked back, I could see her looking at me. I could not understand and wondered what she was thinking.

During this time, my girlfriend Ellen had received Alabaster oil from TBN as a partner. She worked at the Department of Labor, and would come to the hospital on her lunch hour everyday to anoint Faith. This was what God had instructed her to do.

On August 22, 2003, Faith was scheduled for surgery to have the tracheotomy tube placed in her throat. I arrived at the hospital one hour before the surgery. To my dismay, they told me she could not have surgery because she was in distress. I became angry because no one had called me. I did not expect to hear this disturbing news, which turned my world upside down. Before coming to the hospital I thought everything was fine and Wham! Everything had changed again. I became perplexed wondering what was going on.

The ventilator was turned up, and the doctors said Faith's kidneys were shutting down. She seemed to have more phlegm in her lungs, and the nurse was often suctioning it out. I could not take my eyes off of the machines or my daughter, hoping for a miracle. I sat by her bed as the moments passed, listening to the constant, upsetting beeps and buzzes that made me shudder. I watched the commotion as nurses and doctors came in. The ventilator and the medication were preventing me from communicating with my baby.

My husband and I and our son Justin stayed at the hospital. The social worker came in and tried to prepare me for her death. However, I still wanted my daughter to live.

Since spending time with Faith in the hospital, some

children had died, and some had gotten better. I began to listen to those around me. A mother was crying because she wanted her son to live. A mother rejoiced because her daughter was going to make it. We were all different, but yet the same--each wanting our child to recover.

My husband and I stood outside the waiting room. We heard a father crying because his son was in an accident, and they did not know if he would make it. Although my husband and I were going through our own turmoil, we asked the family if we could pray for them. My husband prayed, and I hugged the mother before going into a waiting room around the corner.

At 10:00 that night, the mother of the child that we had prayed for came running to me. "Nicolas is dead," she cried. I hugged her, and we knelt on the floor in the foyer of the hospital crying. She began to talk about how special her son was. I told her to hold on to the memories. After Nicolas's family left, the waiting room was empty. I reclined in a chair and drifted off to sleep.

The doctor came to get us at 5:00 a.m. Faith had gone into cardiac arrest and needed resuscitation. I walked in and saw them pounding on my little girl's chest, and they got a heart beat back. The doctor then approached us with a grim look on her face, and said, "We need to talk." We stood outside of Faith's room.

"Mr. and Mrs. Hinnant," the doctor continued, "you have to make a decision. If Faith goes into cardiac arrest again, what do you want us to do? We can either withdraw care or do all we can to save her life."

I did not want them to withdraw care. I felt that meant I was giving up. My husband looked at me.

"Libby," he said, "what do you want to do?"

"Honey," I answered, "please...let's keep fighting. She

is stable now. Let's just wait and see before we make a decision."

The Unexpected

∞∞∞

Blessed are they that mourn: for they shall be comforted.
Matthew 5:4

The sun was just coming up, yet it was to be the darkest day of my life. My husband and I and my son were the only ones in the waiting room. The nurse came to get us at 6:45 a.m. They said Faith was going into cardiac arrest again. I walked into her room sobbing and crying. A sinking feeling of dread slowly moved over me. I walked into the room as my daughter was dying. I was crying because I had no control over her life.

"Libby," my husband whispered in my ear, "let her go."

"I can't...I can't," I said. I walked in and stood by her bedside and began to talk to her. I told her how much I loved her, and that she had brought so much joy to my life.

I then said, "Faith, if you want to go home with Jesus, you can. Elder Shorter died and went to heaven the other day." *(Elder Shorter served as youth pastor. He and Faith had a spiritual bond).* When I told her about Elder Shorter a teardrop fell from her eyes. Then I said, "You can go."

Faith's heart rate immediately dropped to zero, and I watched as the line on the monitor screen went flat. I felt, once again, as if my heart was being ripped out. I will never forget that moment and that day. And I also remember the day as the day that the unexpected happened.

My husband began singing to Faith, "I'll see you again on the other side." I suddenly became frantic because Justin had not said good-bye. While my husband was singing, a heart rate registered on the monitor! I immediately went to get Justin from the waiting room. He came and kissed his sister and cried. My husband and I and our son, Justin, stood by Faith's bedside holding each other. I looked down on my daughter's dead body that had been ravaged by AIDS. Her body was no longer swollen her skin had a beautiful glow. Faith looked so peaceful.

Yet, we all suffered a deep loss that day. My husband and I lost our daughter, and Justin lost a sister. A part of our lives was taken. I bent down and gave Faith a kiss. She still felt warm.

We went back into the waiting room. My husband began to call the family to let them know that she was gone. The nurse came in and asked if we wanted to hold her.

"I can't," I cried. "I killed her."

My husband said he wanted to hold his baby. We went back into the room. There was no sound of machines. Everything was turned off, and the tubes were disconnected from her body. Samuel lifted Faith from the bed and rocked her one last time. He rocked her for about thirty minutes. He held her close and sang, and I rubbed her head and touched her face. Her skin still felt warm. I remembered the joy she brought to our lives.

At that moment, my thoughts drifted to the day she was born. In the delivery room, my husband Samuel had lifted Faith up to God and said, "Lord, we give our child back to You. Use her for Your glory."

I asked myself--was *this* for God's glory? Our baby had fought so long and so hard. She deserved to be with Jesus. Yet, the pain I felt was beyond description. How could I describe the suffocating depths of pain, suffering, and agony I felt as I watched my child die before my eyes.

Shortly thereafter, my brother-in-law Glenn and his wife Jeannette arrived at the hospital. They had done their best to prepare us for this day. A few weeks earlier Glenn came to the hospital to visit Faith. He looked at me and said "are you prepared" I quickly dismissed the notion. However, they knew Faith was dying. I admit I was not prepared. I had expected her to recover. I had released Faith that morning when I said "if you want to go home to Jesus you can.

My husband and I had prayed for healing with all our hearts, and it hadn't happened. In fact, the exact opposite happened. Our child was not healed. I grieved over the loss of my daughter with guilt and remorse. The desire of our hearts was not granted-- at least not to our satisfaction. I had played scriptures that constantly quoted the promises of God.

Our dreams of Faith's growing up, marrying, and having children all blew up in our faces. How could I keep from being angry, bitter and blaming God? I felt empty and the pain was like being cut open and having something of great value taken out. I looked around and realized that Faith was no longer a part of my life on earth. This unspeakable change left nothing the same, not even me.

My friend Julia and my sister-in-law Jeanette began to make funeral arrangements. Donations were given to help with the funeral. I could not handle the details. God had connected Julia and me supernaturally. I felt she was on an assignment from God. For two months, she had come to the hospital every morning, after getting off work.

On August 30, 2003, Faith's home-going service was held at the Greater Lighthouse Church in Lanham, Maryland. The Public viewing was held followed by the funeral. I sat on the front row thinking about the last time she stood where her casket laid singing "Alabaster box." The church was filled to overflowing with people who came to view her body and attend her funeral. Before the funeral, our family stood at her casket crying. I stood viewing her body one last time. It hurt so bad knowing that her casket was about to be closed. I leaned over in the casket touching her firm cold skin. I kissed my baby girl goodbye wailing through my tears.

The funeral began and I wondered how my husband could have the strength to do the eulogy. I sat and listened to testimonies that came from the seeds of harvest planted by little Faith Nicole. She touched so many lives through the life she lived.

Members of the medical staff from Children's Hospital in Washington, D.C. attended in full numbers. Faith's classmates made homemade cards of sympathy and remembrance. The children's dance team danced to her favorite song, "Good- bye World". Faith's god-brother sang "I will lift up my eyes unto the hills," as he had never sung it before. During the service, I played a recording of Faith singing Alabaster Box. The words, "you don't know the cost of the oil in my alabaster box" gave me comfort. I looked and could see the many lives she touched through her short life span.

My husband did the eulogy for his precious daughter Faith. I was astounded as he preached under the anointing and the power of the Holy Spirit. Many lives were changed, including the life of a nurse who rededicated her life to Christ. Numerous comments were made about Faith's loving spirit, and about how much she loved God and others.

A Tribute by Jackie Roy

What can I say about this little girl? Well, she was such a great inspiration to me. I would look at her life and say Wow! What a bold little girl. The way she carried herself was unique. She would always sing praises to her God. She wasn't shy at all. She would encourage you. She was willing to do anything to help out in the church. She had such a love for God--I am sure she would talk to Him and He would talk with her. I believe she really had a relationship with Him that no one really knew about. She had such a meek spirit, but stood tall inside. Even though she was going through a lot, I never saw her give up or heard of her doing so. She trusted God to the end. She had such wisdom for someone her age. She led others to Christ. Some of the young people in the church, especially my daughter Phillicia, really admired her. If no one else would follow Christ, she would. I was really hurt when she left this earth, although I knew she was with Jesus, it was a bit overwhelming for me. Faith is truly greatly missed. From time to time, I still think about her, and when I hear the song "Alabaster Box," tears come to my eyes. I can see her in front of the church singing her little heart out. Her life is a legacy to all she touched. Rest in peace, Faith. I will see you again!

A Tribute by Godmother Ann H. Davis

August 30, 2003

When Faith was born I felt highly honored and privileged--that out of all of her family, saints, and friends--I was asked to be her godmother. Faith was such a precious, friendly little girl all of her life. Her godfather said she was a dedicated person who loved her church. She also loved her family and friends, but most of all she loved her Savior. Faith lived out Romans 1:16 which says, "For I am not ashamed of the gospel of Christ: for it is the power of God." In the hospital Faith was not ashamed; at home, she was not ashamed; at church, she was not ashamed. And now she is with our Savior. I will miss her!

A Poem for Little Faith

For God so loved Faith,
He took her home to keep her safe.
She was a tiny little angel full, of love,
a gift from God above.
He saw her suffering and pain.
She was His before she was yours.
Now she can rest with no more illness.
Everyone will miss her--such a precious gift.
Full of innocence and joy, her burden is lifted.
Remember her spirit; remember her smile.
So you can rest now little Faith.
God has come and prepared a place.

--Written by cousin Natisha Green

A Tribute by Aunt Emma Hinnant

I always look toward heaven, and I wonder why so many things happen. I guess it's all for a purpose, a purpose why you live and why you die. Faith life brought so much love, joy, and spiritual comfort to us all. It brought me such pain when I heard you had gone to live with the King. Memories shot through my mind. When I close my eyes I see you there, just prancing around--the little praise dancer you were, praising her Lord in motion. I'll always miss your poetry recitals on the phone, just you and me and the Lord. Our phone calls brought joy to me when I was depressed; you lifted my spirit (KID, YOU WERE GOOD, A TRUE CHILD OF GOD). Faith, you will always be in our hearts, minds, and souls.

Words spoke by Faith and recorded by Emma Hinnant

"Lord Jesus, I just love, I Just love you. I just know I love you, Lord Jesus. I just love you.

Jesus in my life and He won't let me go; Jesus in my life and He won't let me go. Jesus won't let me go.

I love you on the way to your house. Jesus won't let me go. Every time He won't let me go, and I love you, and I love you. He just won't let me go."

From Pain to Gain

∞∞∞

In this you greatly rejoice, though now for a little while, if need be, you have been grieved by various trials, that the genuineness of your faith, being much more precious than gold that perishes,...
1 Peter 1:6-7 (NKJV)

We buried Faith on August 30, 2003, on a hot summer day. On that day, I began to feel the hard reality that my life was now empty and sad. I needed God's grace to help me in my weakness and times of grief. I found strength in Hebrews 4:15-16 "Let us therefore come boldly unto the throne of grace that we may obtain mercy, and find grace to help in time of need."

In the first year following Faith's death, experiencing her birthday and all the holidays without her was the toughest. I lived through days and nights of tears and sadness. Death had invaded our family circle, and a part of our family was gone. The basic routine of getting out of bed and walking past her room or of driving past her school all brought tears and sadness to my heart. The wound was fresh and unprocessed. I just could not seem to move on.

A few months following Faith's death Justin moved to South Carolina to attend college. Justin said he was angry and could not cry. In the past many times Justin saw the pain that Faith and I suffered. I now wanted to spare him the pain of watching me grieve.

The pain of Faith's death was incomprehensible, and

there were no words to describe it. I longed for a normal life; yet, during this season the abnormal became normal. I could not sleep. I shed tears night and day. I relived her last days in my mind, wishing they had never happened. And wrapped up in my pain was the burden of guilt. When I went to church and saw other children her age, I grieved inwardly because I missed my child. I remembered carrying her in my womb, nurturing, and loving her. I dreamed of her life on earth and grieved that death took that dream away.

The sorrow I felt was like a deep wound, a pain so deep it could not be articulated. Time dragged, with days feeling like weeks, weeks like months, and months like years. Samuel and I constantly yearned inwardly, feeling our loss, and wanting our daughter back in our lives. I tried to push the hurt away, but could not. The hurt was inside; it could not be pushed away, nor concealed.

Nine months after Faith's death, I faced my first Mother's Day without her. I remember going to the cemetery that day and just sitting in the car crying overcome with so much grief that I could not get out the car. A month later was Father's Day, no less painful. As we got ready for church, Samuel took the last Father's day card he had gotten from Faith out of the dresser drawer. Shaking his head, he murmured, "I miss my baby." I then reminisced on how determined Faith was to get her father this card.

She was in the hospital at the time and asked me to take her to the gift shop. I put her in a wheelchair and took her to the gift shop, not knowing it would be the last time she would be picking out a Father's Day card. She found a card for her father and signed it Daddy's little girl.

Despite our sadness and pain, we went to church on that first Father's Day after Faith's death. During the service

Yolanda, the pastor's daughter walked with me into the hall. She began telling me that God had laid it on her heart to ask my husband Samuel to be a father to her daughter Shante, since Shante's father was not in her life. My spirit quickly agreed. Before the close of the service, Yolanda and her daughter Shante stood and asked Samuel publicly to take the role of Shante's father. Samuel was surprised and in awe as tears flowed down his face. On that day, he hugged Shante and received her as his daughter. She became daddy's little girl and an important part of Samuel's, Justin's and my life. My husband often said the things we so missed seeing and experiencing with Faith were to experience with Shante. My husband and I shared the joy of her graduating from high school and other accomplishments.

As time passed, we began to move forward. I went through several phases of grief after my daughter's death, and each phase enabled me to progress. The first stage involved active recollection and longing for the pleasures of our past together. In the second stage, I remembered and reviewed the impact of Faith Nicole's life and death. The third stage brought me to the place of resolving to live out the rest of my life for God with the strength He would provide. I began to thank God for the time He allowed Faith Nicole to be in our lives.

However, about the time I was healing from the pain of losing Faith Nicole, fresh pain entered my life. In July 2004 my mother Donella became ill and was hospitalized. My husband and I drove to South Carolina, where my mother lived. On that weekend, July 29, 2004, my mother was diagnosed with pancreatic cancer and given six months to live. She was sixty-six years old.

Pancreatic cancer is considered one of the worst kinds of

cancer because it is so difficult to diagnose. My mother had had chronic pain in her stomach, but although she went to the emergency room several times and had received numerous tests and ultra sounds, the doctors told her there was nothing wrong and sent her home every time. Now, along with facing the loss of my mother, I faced the challenge of losing a key person who helped keep Faith's memory alive. Both Faith's and my mother's birthdays were on November 5.

About a month after learning about my mother's diagnosis, I visited Faith's grave site. It was August 23, 2004, a year after Faith's death. I remember standing at her grave site--thanking God for the time He had allowed Faith to be in our lives. My heart became filled with gratitude for the years she had been with us. On that same day, I took flowers to the pediatric intensive care unit and to the nursing unit floor. I also visited Faith's doctors. Doctor Spegial, one of her doctors, said Faith had been an inspiration. In fact, since her death he had gone to Africa to give medical care to children with AIDS. He showed my husband and me the slide show of his trip to Africa.

Three months later, on November 5, I celebrated Faith's birthday and memory. As part of this, I accepted an invitation to speak at a fund raising banquet to help families dealing with HIV. The banquet was held on November 5, Faith's birth date. This speaking engagement was made even harder by the recent news of my mother's cancer. However, it brought sunshine in my pain to think of others. In November 2004, my husband received his credentials to serve as a pastor. Samuel began praying and seeking God's direction concerning ministry. A few months later, we moved back to South Carolina to start Hands of hope and Faith Ministries. During this time, my mother's health declined.

On New Year's Eve 2005, as my brother Jerry and I were walking our mother down the hall, I turned to Mom and said, "Mom it is 2005 and you made it."

She looked at me with her weak eyes and said, "Quitters don't win." I held her words close to my heart because I knew her time was near. Those words gave me strength. I felt if my mother could look at death and say "quitters don't win," I could be inspired not to quit.

A few weeks later on January 13, 2005, my mother died. I knew my mother and daughter were out of pain and with God. Yet sorrow once again tried to fill my life. Then I remembered my mother's words and I was inspired not to quit.

After my mother's death, my husband and I decided to stay in South Carolina permanently. It was a time of adjustment, and we were seeking God's will for our lives.

The Lord used Christian television as a means of strength and encouragement during this time. I heard Juanita Bynum preach a message on the topic of being born for ministry. After hearing , a powerful anointing came through the television into my room. I began to pray in the spirit for my ministry . As I prayed in the spirit, I heard my daughter say "Mommy... is for the greater." I did not understand.

On another occasion, late one night I was watching TBN and listening to Harry, and Cheryl Salem speak about the death of their daughter. The words they spoke connected with words spoken in my spirit about it being "for the greater." The Salems began to share about how their daughter was not a part of their past, but their future. Through this revelation, I began to see Faith in our future. I began to see her in our ministries--in every sermon, we would preach, and in every life, we would touch. I began to glory in my tribulation, recalling Romans 5:3-4 "And not only so, but we glory in tribulations also: knowing that tribulation worketh patience; And patience, experience; and experience, hope."

One day, as God continued the process of extracting grief and despair out of my broken heart, He brought these words from Isaiah 53:4 to mind: "Surely he hath borne our griefs, and carried our sorrows." I felt the Spirit of God, who had seemed to lie dormant for so long, come alive inside. I felt that familiar hand applying gentle pressure in my inner being, pressing me to step out and see what God might do.

On August 23, 2005, two years after Faith's death, I got dressed to go to her grave site. In my mind, I was going to her grave to grieve, and I felt I had the right. But the Holy Spirit within me declared *enough is enough…she is not there*. More and more, the Lord helped me to move beyond my grief and to live a more normal life again.

The Lord granted encouragement and inspiration along the way in a variety of ways, and often through music. A couple of songs He used to help give me courage to move beyond my pain were "In My Daughter's Eyes," by Martina McBride, and "Trading My Sorrows," by Darrell Evans.

In 2005, two years after my daughter's death and seven months after my mother's death, I sensed in my heart and mind that I was beginning to emerge from a time of darkness. Increasingly, I was being drawn by God's Spirit through the power of Almighty God, out of the horrible pit of despair. I also began to grow in my understanding that Faith was not in my past but my future, and that Samuel and I were indeed moving together from pain to gain. That doesn't mean trials have ceased.

On Mother's Day 2008, my husband suffered a stroke

that affected his left side. However, through Jesus Christ, he has received the victory with minimal damage. We continue to believe God for total restoration. And we continue to seek God's direction for ministry paths where we can exalt Him and where He can use the pain we've experienced to point others to Him. Samuel and I have a deep yearning to reach out to the lost and hurting. For a time in 2005, this was fulfilled through a radio broadcast we started, *The Hands of Hope and Faith.* We also began seeking a local place of worship in our new location. In 2007 we joined the Saint John's Progressive church family under the leadership of Pastor Gloria Cooper.

When I reflect on the deep pain the Lord has allowed in my life, the Apostle Paul's words come to mind: "Nay, in all these things," he reminds us, "we are more than conquerors through him that loved us. For I am persuaded," he writes, "that neither death, nor life, nor angels, nor principalities, nor powers, nor things present, nor things to come, Nor height, nor depth, nor any other creature, shall be able to separate us from the love of God, which is in Christ Jesus our Lord"(Romans 8:37-39).

Yes, trials will continue until the day we see Jesus Christ face-to-face. Yet looking back, I can see that the trials the Lord has allowed in my life have made me strong, teaching me His ways. And I rejoice that God in His mercy has taken the shattered pieces of my life and made me whole again. I praise Him for His sustaining grace as He has guided the footsteps of a miracle in my life here on earth.

As the time passed, we continued to move forward while Samuel and I experienced the restoration power of God in our lives. " He restoreth my soul"(Psalms 23:3). I experienced healing in my body and Samuel overcame a stroke in 2008. This was a reality for us "For I will restore health unto thee, and I will heal thee of thy wounds." (Jeremiah 30:7)

I went from pain to gain in Jesus Christ and from this experience God used our pain to give hope and faith to others. Together with Samuel, we tasted God's goodness, which filled our hearts with love and gratitude. Samuel, a Pastor and great man of faith, started Hands of Hope and Faith Ministry in our home.

We broadcasted on the radio with sermons and had a prayer phone line to pray with others. We also went into the homes of the sick and hurting. We later work on ministerial staff with Living Water Ministry after my brother has a stroke, we work with my brother We moved from Pain to Gain in Christ Jesus.

Blind -Sided
Pot Holes on the Road of Life

∞∞∞

Isaiah 41:13 KJV For I Lord thy God will hold thy right hand, saying unto thee, Fear not; I will help thee.

The years passed, and the power of God healed my heart. Although the road to healing was not easy, I was grateful that God gave me Samuel, who loved me unconditionally. Through the years, I valued our relationship as husband and wife as we served in ministry unto the Lord and committed our plans to Him.

However, on May 18, 2014, one day before Samuel's 59th birthday, while we were driving to a funeral, we were in a car accident. As a result, we were blind-sided by the unexpected. Samuel was injured and taken to the hospital. The doctor ordered a MRI which showed a mass on his liver and spleen. Later, a biopsy revealed he had a rare form of liver cancer. However, the doctors said that surgery might be an option.

After hearing the diagnosis of cancer, it weighed me down. I tried to process the news, and my mind became filled with intrusive thoughts that I would watch my husband die. Samuel discerned my thoughts and said "do not go there." Samuel later called Mother Ann Davis, our mother in Christ, and told her he had cancer of the liver. She was shocked, but immediately said "it's God's liver;" and he readily agreed. I then responded as Paul writes, "Casting down imaginations, and every high thing that exalteth itself against the knowledge of God, and bringing into captivity every thought to the obedience of Christ; (II Corinthians 10:5). I decided to get my thoughts in line with the Word of God and believe that Samuel would be healed.

Two weeks later, the doctor referred Samuel to Duke's Hospital in Durham, North Carolina to determine if he could be a candidate for a liver transplant. While we waited for the scheduled appointment, we reached out for prayer from family and friends. The night before, church members and family came to our home and prayed with us. After the prayer, I felt at peace knowing others were praying for us.

On the morning of the appointment, Samuel and I traveled with our son Justin for three hours to the hospital in Durham, North Carolina to see the doctor. I drove because Samuel was tired. While driving, I thought about how earlier I had to shower him because he was too weak, and I felt his body come down on me. Now, I felt the spiritual heaviness of the attack against his body. Inwardly I began to pray for healing and restoration. When I was sick and at my lowest, I recalled Samuel's words to me "your sickness is not unto death." Now, I declared that Samuel would live and not die.

We finally arrived at the hospital, and I walked into the doctor's office filled with hope. The doctor introduced himself and began to tell us he reviewed the x-rays and the MRI. He informed us that the prognosis was not good and said, "Mr. Hinnant cancer is in your liver and spleen." Immediately, those words gripped my heart, and I burst into tears.

Through my tears, I asked the question slowly with my lips trembling, "how long does he have to live"? Holding my breath and my heart beating fast, the doctor answered, "you may have six months or less to live." At that moment, our eyes met in disbelief. The unanticipated prognosis shook me to the core of my being. Hearing his life expectancy was too much to handle. The dream I had of us growing old together shattered in my mind. Despite the prognosis, the doctor admitted Samuel to the hospital for further testing to get a liver transplant.

We were facing the unexpected, and I needed to trust God. I wanted to, but it was hard. I found myself looking at my past losses rather than God. However, Samuel declared the doctors did not have the last say.

As I sat by his bedside, I listened as he called and told others about his condition, and fear pierced my heart. Samuel looked at me and said, "everything is going to be alright." However, I was still trying to process how long the doctor said he had to live.

I later thought about how our day was supposed to go, but now everything changed. Months before finding out that Samuel had cancer, he began planning a family reunion for the Hinnant family. We made the reservations for the hotel, and he looked forward to seeing his family coming from out of town.

However, I was left not knowing what to do. Samuel said he would be okay, and he wanted me to go and complete the details. I then agreed, reminding myself of the words my daughter Faith Nicole, who said before her death, "the devil still doesn't win."

The next day my son and I traveled for two hours from Durham, North Carolina, to Wilson, North Carolina, where the reunion would be held. After arriving, I completed the reunion details. Later that night at dinner I shared the news of Samuel's condition. I also called Samuel, and he talked with his brothers and sisters. Plans for the weekend included a visit to The Hinnant's ancestors' birthplace and a banquet. However, the plans were changed, for his family and I decided to go to the hospital. We drove in several cars from Wilson, North Carolina, to Durham. While going, I thought of how he would feel seeing his brothers, sisters, nieces, and nephews.

When we arrived at the hospital and walked into his room, a big smile came on his face. My heart filled with joy. I began to thank God for the family reunion that brought his family together. During this visit, we met with the doctors to hear their plans, which were positive and hopeful.

After the visit, we went back to Wilson, North Carolina, and had a family reunion banquet. My heart ached that Samuel was not there.

During the night, I got a call that his condition had worsened. I was upset and crying, and Shante the young lady we helped raised immediately drove me to the hospital. On our way there we both cried and tried to console each other. I began to think about the day when she stood in front of the church and asked Samuel to be her father. I was grateful that she came to the family reunion as part of our family.

When we finally got to the hospital and went to his room, Shante and I hugged and kissed Samuel. I then saw a beautiful smile come over his face. I later talked to the doctors, and they told me he was declining and may only have a few weeks to live. Shante and I stayed by his bedside that night.

The next day the family reunion ended, and his family returned to their homes. However, I stayed at the hospital praying and believing that he could have surgery. Through it all, I was grateful that his family came to spend time with him. I then realized all of this was a part of God's plan, and my heart rejoiced.

After staying by Samuel's bedside for eight days, I went home for one day because his brother Richard came to see him. I left the hospital, and I drove home crying. I then called my friend Jackie, and she prayed for me. We both prayed and believed God for a miracle.

I went back to the hospital. However, on the tenth day, the doctor took me aside and said "we have done all we could." I cried and said, "how can I tell him he is dying." I then asked the doctor to tell Samuel because I felt he had a right to know. I stood on one side of the bed and the doctor on the other. I tried hard not to cry as the doctor said, "Mr. Hinnant we have done all we can." Samuel immediately shifted his eyes from the doctor to me, and my heart dropped.

I later went into the waiting room across the hall, and cried "God this is too much!" I began to call our family and friends who were shocked to learn that the doctors had done all they could and many came to see him. However, my heart became heavy as Samuel grew weaker and stopped talking. I prayed that God would cover his mind and heart. I also prayed that he would not be bitter or angry with God. I prayed asking for peace and assurance about his relationship with Jesus Christ.

On Samuel's 12th day in the hospital, I stood by his bedside with his brother Glenn and friend, Pastor Phillip Roy; and we began to pray in the spirit. During our prayer, Samuel began to pray with us, and my heart rejoiced because this gave me the peace and comfort I needed. Throughout the day, family and friends continued to fill his room. I realized Samuel was getting a return on the love he gave to others. I whispered in his ear, "baby, our family and friends came to see you because they love you."

On the next day, I saw a look in Samuel's eyes, which reminded me of my mother when she passed. Later that day, I went into the chapel to pray. I fell to my knees and asked God for peace and grace to endure. I returned to the room, and my words were few because my heart ached for my husband.

Meanwhile, prayer and worship music filled the room. I told everyone that this time was between Samuel and his Savior Jesus Christ. I then looked at my 6 ft. husband in the hospital bed,and my mind filled with thoughts and my heart filled with emotions. None of this made any sense to me. In my mind I thought to myself this is the man that God brought to me. I thought of how he boldly proclaimed to me when I was sick that my sickness was not unto death, and God told him I was to be his wife. Now 23 years later I am looking at him wondering will he live or will he die.

Around 11:00 p.m. Samuel began to struggle between life and death. Then, I got in bed with him and laid my head on his chest with my arms around his body. Tears were flowing, and I said, "Sammy, I love you. I will be okay. God will take care of me." I held my head up and watched him say his final words "I love you." Then Samuel took his last breath, and the doctor pronounced him dead at 11:45 p.m. Together I stood with family and friends as we looked at his lifeless body. We struggled with the realization that Samuel had died.

Walking out of the hospital that night, I felt emotionally drained. We went and stayed in a hotel for the night. I found myself crying throughout the night. However, I found peace in Samuel's final days because he spent time with his son Justin, brothers, sisters, godson Shaquan, Shante, nieces, nephews, brothers, sisters-in-law and friends.

The following day my family and friends from Maryland went to their homes, and my sisters came to drive home to South Carolina. During this three-hour drive, I thought about Samuel's thirteen days in the hospital. My heart ached for my son Justin losing his stepfather. He already experienced the loss of his biological father, sister, and brother. I wondered how this loss would affect him. I wanted to shield him from pain.

When I arrived home, I made arrangements for Samuel's body to be brought back home. Then I began the heart-wrenching ordeal of planning his funeral. Plans were for a viewing service in South Carolina and a funeral in Maryland.

Finally, the day of the funeral came, and we drove from South Carolina to Maryland. When I entered the church and saw the casket, my mind went back to the day that our daughter Faith Nicole's casket was in that same place. I then walked up with Justin by my side to view Samuel's body, and my legs became weak. I cried from the deepest part of my being. I stood looking down on his body, overcome with the reality that death took my husband of 23 years of marriage.

I sat through the service listening to special tributes given by those who knew and loved him. Justin wrote a poem about his father. Shante did a tribute and a special salute. Also, our Godson Shaquan, sang a song in the anointing. The eulogy was done by Pastor Phillip Roy. After the service was over, God granted my heart desires and I buried Samuel beside our daughter Faith Nicole.

I stayed in Maryland for a while with friends and later returned to South Carolina with feelings of uncertainty. I grieved the loss of my parents, my son, Dwayne my daughter, Faith and my first husband. However, I discovered that grief is not just one type of feeling. Samuel's death obstructed my life so much that I could not determine what was next without him.

With Samuel's death weighing heavily on me, I asked myself "can I get through this?" I felt like my life had turned to ashes. I still functioned in ministry, preaching and serving God. I cried out to God because I did not understand why. Satan began to use the memories of the death of all my loved ones to bring me down and fill my life with added pain.

I continued through the pain, remembering what Samuel said to me "keep preaching." I fought the enemy of my soul and asked God's help to move forward and help to fulfill His call on my life.

Moving Forward

∞∞∞

He healeth the broken in heart, and bindeth up their wounds. Psalms 147:3

One year after the death of Samuel, The Holy Spirit began to bring order in my life. I started experiencing emotional healing through my relationship with Jesus Christ, my Advocate, Helper, and Counselor. The words of Jesus Christ gave me rest. "Come unto me, all [ye] that labour and are heavy laden, and I will give you rest." (Matthew 11:28) Throughout my life, the power of Jesus Christ healed my broken heart as the scripture says, " He healeth the broken in heart,and bindeth up their wound."(Psalm 147:3)

I continued in ministry preaching as, God's grace covered me at my weakest point. As Paul writes, "My grace is sufficient for you, for My strength is made perfect in weakness" (II Corinthians 12:9.) I prayed for God's strength to empower me to keep pushing and pressing on.

A pivotal point in my healing began with a sermon entitled "First Things First" focusing on the scripture, "Thou shalt love the Lord thy God with all thy heart, and with all thy soul, and with all thy strength, and with all thy mind; and thy neighbor as thyself." (Luke 10:27)

I once again shook the devil off and determined defeat was not an option. My faith stirred, and God reminded me that He came through in my toughest battle between life and death. I began to rise above the ashes of defeat, and God began to give me joy for mourning as the scripture declares ...to give unto them beauty for ashes, the oil of joy for mourning, the garment of praise for the spirit of heaviness; (Isaiah 61:3)

Throughout my writing, I have shared openly with truth and transparency. I have not written this book out of a desire for empathy or sympathy but to encourage you to hold on no matter the circumstances. I do not have the testimony of instant healing, and I do not have the testimony of always being on the mountaintop. I write as a believer who sometimes felt like giving up; however, I decided to stay in the race.

During my struggles, I thought of great witnesses in the Bible. These witnesses inspired me and gave me hope and courage. Stephen echoed victory in Christ while being stoned to death. Paul finished his course at the appointed time. Moses contended that he would lead the people out of Egypt despite Pharaoh's attempts to stop him.

Throughout my life I faced many curves and turns. It was not easy. I cried, laughed, sang, sighed, and mourned along the way. Sometimes, I could not comprehend how God could use my life story as a blessing to others. Despite my feelings the Lord encouraged me to put one foot in front of the other. Whenever I fell, I got up and kept walking. It worked.

At times the devil fought me in the realm of my emotions. I saw myself as a runner with my eyes glued to the finish line. I was in a race, and as I ran toward the finish line through pain and tears, remembering, "I can do all things through Christ, which strengtheneth me (Philippians 4:13).

I long ago decided to openly share my battles and victories with others and give God the glory. Only God Almighty Himself could have brought me out of that horrible pit. "He brought me up also out of an horrible pit, out of the miry clay, and set my feet upon a rock, and established my goings" (Psalm 40:2).

I make no claims to passing every test, but I seek to do the will of God. I know that Jesus Christ is my Advocate and I can depend on Him in every circumstance.

When I finished writing this book, the devil attacked me. saying "What if you get sick and die?" he taunted.

"Satan, have you forgotten?" I replied. "I have already laid my life down at the feet of Jesus. So if I perish, I perish. Hallelujah!"

Every chapter in this book represents a footprint of God's miracle-working power in my life. I wrote about the obstacles that came against me to keep me from my miracle. I have written to encourage every reader to hold on to the promises of God.

My expectations are from God, and my desires are found in His Word. I have not arrived, but I am pressing toward the mark. "Brethren," God's Word says, "I count not myself to have apprehended: but this one thing I do, forgetting those things which are behind, and reaching forth unto those things which are before, I press toward the mark for the prize of the high calling of God in Christ Jesus" (Phil. 3:13).

I consider the next pages of this book the most crucial of all because they point to the conclusion of it all--what matters most and the key to finding that. Through the power of the Holy Spirit, I pray that God will come through these pages and meet you at your point of need. No matter what we go through in life, we are more than conquerors through Him. I have discovered that Jesus waits to bless us as we wander around in the "wilderness."

Satan's goal is to keep you from God. Someone reading this book may say, "I don't want to come to Jesus in my low estate." Remember, as Jesus was dying on the cross, the thief cried out "save me" at the last hour. It's not too late.

God desires to give you peace: "And the peace of God, which passeth all understanding, shall keep your hearts and minds through Christ Jesus" (Phil. 4:7). Sin has destroyed many lives. Sin separates us from God.

Only Jesus Himself can stop the spiritual decay of sin. "For the wages of sin is death; but the gift of God is eternal life through Jesus Christ our Lord." (Romans 6:23).

God has made His plan of salvation accessible to all--from the youngest, like our Faith Nicole--to the most elderly among us. The invitation extends to all.

The Bible tells us that God loves us and died for us. "For God so loved the world, that he gave his only begotten Son, that whosoever believeth in him should not perish, but have everlasting life" (John 3:16)

In order to become a child of God, a person must recognize the need for a Savior and be willing to accept God's free gift of salvation: "For the wages of sin is death; but the gift of God is eternal life through Jesus Christ our Lord." (Rom. 6:23).

My dear reader, if you are reading this book and recognize your need for a Savior, understand that God has made a way for you. Christ died for your sins. According to 2 Corinthians 5:15, "He died for all, that they which live should not henceforth live unto themselves, but unto him which died for them, and rose again . The Bible is clear in teaching that Jesus is the only way. "Jesus saith unto him, I am the way, the truth, and the life: no man cometh unto the Father, but by me (John 14:6).

My prayer as the author of this book is that God in his infinite love would minister His healing mercy and grace..

Secrets of the Journey

∞∞∞

Remembering mine affliction and my misery, the wormwood and the gall. My soul hath them still in remembrance, and is humbled in me. This I recall to my mind, therefore have I hope. It is of the LORD'S mercies that we are not consumed, because his compassions fail not. They are new every morning: great is thy faithfulness.
Lamentations 3:19-23

The entire foundation of my journey as I have gone from footprint to footprint, has been that of God Himself doing His work in me. His grace brought changes in my heart and my life. In every step I have relied on God's grace to make it. I credit His grace for transforming my thinking and renewing my mind.

In this closing chapter of *Footprints* to *a Miracle,* I will share a few reflections of my journey and lessons learned--lessons I have sometimes revisited to maintain victory in my life.

1. Come clean before God.

This is truly an ongoing process. In times of trouble, we find we can't fake our way. I know I couldn't. I dealt with the issue of knowing God deeply and honestly. On my living room floor, as I lay prostrate before God, He instructed me to take off my spiritual mask and get to know Him.

2. Be forgiving and repentant.

An unforgiving spirit ties the hand of God. "And when

ye stand praying," we are reminded in Mark 11:25, "forgive, if ye have ought against any: that your Father also which is in heaven may forgive you your trespasses". The person who had wronged me was dead, but I was still obligated to forgive him.

3. Build yourself up on your most holy faith.

Jude 1:20-21 exhorts us, "But ye, beloved, building up yourselves on your most holy faith, praying in the Holy Ghost, Keep yourselves in the love of God, looking for the mercy of our Lord Jesus Christ unto eternal life".

I can never express adequately how the weapon of praying in the Holy Ghost kept me as I walked towards my footprints of a miracle. I always had the privilege of praying to my Father in my heavenly language, and the devil could not get in on our conversations. This is where the deep things of God are revealed. This is where I could lay on the spiritual operating table and God could have His way with me.

4. Give God's Word first place.

"Wherewithal shall a young man cleanse his way? by taking heed thereto according to thy word. With my whole heart have I sought thee: O let me not wander from thy commandments" (Psalm 119:9-10).

I searched the Scriptures for comfort in my times of testing. God gave me personal insight through His word, and His Word gave light to my path.

5. Turn your face to seek the Lord.

I found myself getting into the habit, more and more, of seeking God in every turn of events I faced. Sometimes this involved making an about face--reversing a direction I was going in--and allowing God to redirect my steps. A verse in Job comes to mind: "I would seek unto God, and unto God would I commit my cause" (Job 5:8).

6. Encourage yourself.

When my spirit was cast down, I often thought of David's experience, and these words from Psalm 42 encouraged my own soul: "Why art thou cast down, O my soul? and why art thou disquieted in me? hope thou in God: for I shall yet praise him for the help of his countenance" (Psalm 42:5).

7. Let God surround you with songs of deliverance

I recall two songs that especially gave me comfort in the midst of my grief, and the AIDS diagnosis. One of them was "The Joy of the Lord is my Strength." I realized I needed joy--not the kind of joy that I would try to drum up--but true inner joy that only the Lord could provide. The other song was "Lord, Don't Let Me Fail." This song reminded me that the Lord was always near, always walking "right by my side" supporting me and giving me strength.

I encourage you to find your song in the midst of trial--the song that reaches down into the pit of your pain and pulls you out.

8. Look to God and not the problem.

I learned to take my eyes off of my problems and human weakness and turn my focus to Jesus instead: "Looking unto Jesus the author and finisher of our faith; who for the joy that was set before him endured the cross, despising the shame, and is set down at the right hand of the throne of God" (Heb. 12:2).

9. Let God reveal to you those that will walk with you with the spirit of Caleb and Joshua.

The Lord impressed on me the importance of surrounding myself with those who had deep trust in God, like Joshua and Caleb. Their faith and reliance on God is reflected in Numbers 14:8: "If the LORD delight in us, then he will bring us into this land, and give it us; a land which floweth with milk and honey".

I prayed and asked God to cover me and surround me with those of like faith and those who could increase my faith when it became weakened. Through Christ I have been blessed with doctors, family, and friends who walked with me in confidence and understanding. This became very important on my journey toward my footprints of a miracle.

10. Fight the good fight of faith.

As the Lord granted peace and victory in the footprints along the way, I came to understand more and more that the battle truly does belong to Him. "Ye shall not need to fight in this battle," the Lord declares in 2 Chronicles 20:17, "stand ye still, and see the salvation of the LORD with you, O Judah and Jerusalem: fear not, nor be dismayed; to-morrow go out against them: for the LORD will be with you.

Another verse that shows God going to battle for His people is 2 Chronicles 32:8: "With him [the king of Assyria] is an arm of flesh; but with us is the LORD our God to help us, and to fight our battles. And the people rested themselves upon the words of Hezekiah king of Judah."

This last lesson became especially precious to me after the death of my father--a man who kept the faith throughout his life. In the midst of all his suffering he fought the good fight of faith. And that is my prayer for myself and for all of us.

Father, in the Name of Jesus I thank you for your anointing throughout the pages of this book. I pray that this book has revealed your love. May your Spirit draw many by faith to begin their personal journey of footprints of a miracle.

About the Author

∞∞∞

Olivia is a mother, evangelist and teacher of God's Word. She resides with her family in Florence, South Carolina. Olivia has served in the prison ministry, the radio broadcast, and the nursing home ministry. She has spoken on behalf of several nonprofit organizations.

Olivia's memoir is shared with candor and transparency that invites you into her life. She takes you on a journey filled with bitterness, heartaches and pains.

However, Olivia is willing to share the truth and freedom found in Jesus Christ as her life becomes open to all. Olivia states "my story is important not because it is mine. I write, in truth believing, that my yesterdays can help someone in his or her today.

Through the power of Jesus Christ Olivia overcame the death sentence and did not die. She walks in healing and divine health. She is not bitter but better. She has moved from pain to gain.

Olivia's greatest desire is reaching the lost and those in need. Her desire to reach her destiny being a light pointing to Jesus Christ the Supreme Light. *And let the beauty of the LORD our God be upon us: and establish thou the work of our hands upon us; yea, the work of our hands establish thou it. (Psalm 90:17)*

∞∞∞

Contact Information

Website: oliviahinnantminstries.com
Email:Footprintsofamiracle@gmail.com

∞∞∞

Made in the USA
Columbia, SC
13 January 2024

30415133R00078